Turtmanntal

Visp

BRIG

Stalden

Simplon Pass

St.
Niklaus

Grächen

Saastal

Fletschhorn
Lagginhorn

Saas
Grund

Weissmies

Domodóssola

Mattertal

Nadelhorn

Dom

Saas
Fee

Saas
Almagell

Villa-
dóssola

Täschhorn

Antronapiana

Täsch

Alphubel

Allalinhorn

Val di Antrona

Gabelhorn

Rimpfischhorn

RMATT

Strahlhorn

Piedimulera

horn or
te Cervino

Macugnaga

Valle

MONTE

Dufourspitze
Signalkuppe

Castor
Pollux

C

Rima

acques

Pyramide

Vincent

ROSA

M.Tagliafer

mpoluc

Gres'ney
la Trinité

Alagna
Valsesia

Rimasco

as

Gressoney

Corno
Bianco

Riva
Valdobbia

Balmuccia

Varallo

Brusson

Sesia

ent

Corno Roso

Val

Scopello

Valle

Gres'ney
St. Jean

Valle di

rres

AREA COVERED
BY VOLUME ONE

GW00586033

THE GRAND TOUR
OF MONTE ROSA

A CIRCUIT OF THE PENNINE ALPS

by
Chris Wright

All maps and illustrations by the Author

Volume 1
Martigny to Alagna Valsesia
via the Italian valleys

CICERONE PRESS
MILNTHORPE, CUMBRIA

Designed and Produced
by the author
using an Apple Macintosh©
with Aldus PageMaker™
and Adobe Illustrator™

Cicerone Guides by the same author:
The Westmorland Heritage Walk

Guides by Constable & Company:
A Guide to the Pennine Way
A Guide to the Pilgrims' Way and North Downs Way
A Guide to Offa's Dyke Path
A Guide to the Pembrokeshire Coast Path

Forthcoming:
The Italian Valleys of the Pennine Alps
GTA - The Grand Traverse of the Alps

*Front cover: Monte Tagliaferro, 2964m, rises beyond the Valle d'Otro, seen
from the Bivacco Ravelli, 2504m. (Section 6)*

CONTENTS

VOLUME 1

ADVICE TO READERS

Readers are advised that whilst every effort is taken by the author to ensure the accuracy of this guidebook, changes can occur which may affect the contents. A book of this nature, with detailed descriptions and detailed maps, is more prone to change than a more general guide. Routes can be altered, paths can be eradicated by landslip or forest clearances, footbridges can be washed away in spring floods, waymarking alters, there may be new mountain refuges or old ones closed. It is advisable to check locally on these matters and on transport, accommodation, shops etc. The publisher would welcome notes of any such changes.

THE GRAND TOUR OF MONTE ROSA

Unlike the famous Tour du Mont Blanc, which follows an established route around the highest mountain in Europe and is recognised by the French, Swiss and Italian authorities as an official long-distance footpath (Grande Randonnée), there is, as yet, no official status for The Grand Tour of Monte Rosa (abbreviated in this guide as GTMR).

A circuit of the Monte Rosa range - second only in height to Mont Blanc - has, however, long been possible: settlement in some valleys since the 13thC, packhorse routes over high alpine passes since the 15thC, explorations (mostly by Englishmen) in the 1850s-60s and even new paths created less than thirty years ago, show a history of development of routes that enthusiastic walkers and mountaineers have been able to follow and make their own excursions into and around the range. Unfortunately neither the Union Valaisanne du Tourisme - normally so proficient at waymarking their footpaths - nor the regional tourist associations in Italy - the Azienda Autonoma di Soggiorno e Tourismo (AAST) - have got round to designating the Grand Tour of Monte Rosa and giving it equal status to the Tour du Mont Blanc (although the Italian Alta Via No.1, promoted by the AAST di Aosta, follows part of the GTMR route). (This route also meets, and is followed by, parts of the AVVA No.3 from Ollomont to Cervinia and the GTA - the Grande Traversata delli Alpi - from the Mediterranean coast to Lake Maggiore).

Whereas the Mont Blanc range is often called the 'Western Pennines', and is defined on its eastern side by the deep trench of the Swiss and Italian Ferret valleys, the Central and Eastern Pennines are occupied by a great range of mountains of which the culminating point is Monte Rosa. This range's natural eastern boundary is the Simplon Pass and between the two passes - Col Ferret and Simplon - we may distinguish four groups of mountains divided from each other by the routes over the Col de Chermontane, the St. Théodule and the Monte Moro.

The central range of the Monte Rosa is one of the largest, if not the largest, mountain mass in the Alps and a study of the map shows a marked contrast in the range to that prevailing throughout the adjoining regions. The chain of these Pennine, or Valais, Alps runs west-to-east as the Swiss - Italian frontier. Save in a small part of the Italian valleys the direction of the range and the valleys between them is either parallel or perpendicular to the median. The ridges are very high near the frontier and the deep valleys reach down to the Rhône on the N and the Dora Baltea and the plain of Italy on the S.

Although the summit of Mont Blanc (4807m) overtops by 173m (over 500ft) any peak in the Monte Rosa range the average height of the Monte Rosa group greatly exceeds that of its western rival. The four highest summits of Monte Rosa (the mass is not one individual mountain) surpass 4500m (15,000ft), and three others lie between 4450-4215m (15,000-14,000ft), while within the same limits are the four highest summits of the Saasgrat and the Liskamm, in addition to the neighbouring summits of the Weisshorn, the Matterhorn and the Dent Blanche. The same inference may be drawn from a comparison of the passes, for, with one or two exceptions, all the highest passes in the Alps cross the ridge of the Monte Rosa group. These groups of mountains are divided from each other by the routes over the Col de Chermontane, the St. Théodule and the Monte Moro.

These high passes, whilst affecting a circuit of Monte Rosa for the mountaineer - they are difficult glacier passes demanding ice axe and rope - are outside the scope of the majority. My scheme of the Grand Tour of Monte Rosa is to cross the valleys and their containing ridges as near to the national frontier as possible, and this means the crossing of 'walking' passes sometimes in excess of 3000m (9800ft) or so over the ridges further N or S of the frontier watershed.

In the author's opinion the GTMR is best walked in an anti-clockwise direction. The route is described in fourteen stages or sections: on most sections there are alternative routes over passes of lower altitude, and there are excursions to higher peaks and mountain huts for those that have the ability, experience and time.

This guidebook is published in two volumes. Volume 1 covers the ground between Martigny and Macugnaga, passing mainly via the Italian valleys, while Volume 2 covers the ground between Macugnaga and Martigny, mainly via the Swiss valleys.

To conclude this introduction, I can do no better than quote from a guide to the Alps published at the turn of the century:

"It is the opinion of many of the most competent judges that for grandeur, beauty, and variety the valleys descending from Monte Rosa are entitled to pre-eminence over every other portion of the Alps, and, perhaps, if we regard the union of those three elements, over every other mountain region in the world. Nature is inexhaustible in the combination of her attractions, and certainly there are many other scenes in the Alps which may challenge comparison with whatever is most grand and most beautiful; but no one who would learn thoroughly to enjoy Nature in those aspects cannot do better than give ample time to the exploration of the district. After spending some weeks amid the sterner scenery of Zermatt and Saas, he will find fresh loveliness in the marvellous contrasts that abound in the valleys on the Italian side. A summer's tour devoted to this district, wherein days of exertion, spent in gaining the higher peaks, are made to alternate with days of repose, which need not here be idleness, will certainly not exhaust the beauties of the country, and will probably leave deeper impressions than a rapid excursion extending over a considerable part of the Alps."

THE MONTE ROSA RANGE AND THE PENNINE ALPS

Monte Rosa is a union of four mountain ridges rather than one summit: on plan rather like a four-rayed star or cross. A vast chain stretches generally west to east commencing at the Théodule Pass between Zermatt and Breuil and terminating at the Cima delle Loccie (Punta Grober). This ridge includes the Klein Matterhorn, the Breithorn, Pollux, Castor and Liskamm. Another vast ridge, though a shorter one, meets this nearly at right angles: from the Cima di Jazzi to the N, passing through the four highest summits, to the Pyramide Vincent to the S.

There are seven summits which collectively form the Monte Rosa and they are all at the union or knot formed by these two mountain chains. The fourth highest, and the most conspicuous from the Italian side of the ridge, is the Signalkuppe, 4554m. (It is also called Punta Gnifetti, after the priest of Alagna who first ascended it on 9 August 1842, just three weeks before Forbes' visit to Alagna). The three higher lie all immediately N of Signalkuppe: first in order is the third highest, the Zumsteinspitze, 4563m, a snowy, blunt summit ascended by Zumstein from Gressoney in 1820. A very sharp icy ridge like a house roof leads next to the highest peak, a sharp rocky obelisk on a subsidiary ridge detached from the main ridge, well seen from the Col d'Hérens and from the Monte Moro. Called by von Welden the Hochste Spitze it is now called the Dufourspitze, 4634m, conquered in 1855. The eastern side of the connecting ridge descends with appalling rapidity to an abyss which is scarcely equalled in the Alps for depth or steepness. Beyond Dufourspitze, on the main ridge, is the second highest peak, called by von Welden Nord End, 4609m, first climbed in 1861.

The difference in height of these four summits is a mere 80m, from the highest to the lowest.

Three other summits of somewhat less height form the southern arm of the cross, two on the watershed and political frontier. First is the Parotspitze, 4432m, first climbed in 1863; then the Ludwigshöhe, 4341m, first climbed in 1822; then the Pyramide Vincent, 4215m, first climbed by Vincent, solo, in August 1819. This last, and lowest, completes the Monte Rosa 'tops'.

The northern and western ridges passing through the Monte Rosa 'tops' form the main watershed of the Pennine Alps, a splendid range which is shared between Switzerland and Italy. The northern ridge continues north-east through the Monte Moro to the Simplon while the western continues further west through the Matterhorn and Dent d'Hérens to the Grand St. Bernard Pass.

The lateral valleys that descend from this watershed, in point of individuality and form, and arresting scenery of rock and ice at their culminating heads, yield nothing to those of any other alpine group. Those streams on the Swiss side flow down more or less directly northwards in roughly parallel valleys to join the Rhône; in four cases the streams that enter the Rhône - at Visp, Sierre, Sion and Martigny - are formed by the confluence of two streams that originate in neighbouring parallel valleys. Those streams on the Italian side, on the other hand, for the most part radiate outwards to points ranging eastwards, southwards and south-westwards.

All of these lateral valleys are divided by the magnificent series of ridges which are thrown off the main watershed and these ridges, rather than the valleys, are the dominating features of the Pennine Alps. On these ridges stand some of the grandest and greatest peaks of the Pennine Alps, many of them higher than those standing on the watershed itself.

All of these ridges are crossed by passes, some glacier passes, many lower, leading from valley to valley, which all contribute to the pattern of a continuous traverse around the massif.

Anti-clockwise from the Grand St. Bernard, first on the Italian side and then on the Swiss side of the national frontier, the valleys are:

1. *Valle del Gran San Bernado*

   Carrying the road from the pass through St. Rhémy, Etroubles and Gignod. Gignod is near the junction of the main stream of the Artanavaz, descending from the St. Bernard, with that of the Buthier descending the Val Pelline. Lower down the valley the combined streams meet the Dora Baltea at Aosta.

2. *Valle d'Olomont*

    Draining the S flanks of Mont Velan and the Grand Combin, this short valley joins the Val Pelline at the village of Valpelline.

3. *Val Pelline*

    A long, deeply-cut trench running SW from the Dent d'Hérens, this valley is exactly parallel to the Italian Val Feret that runs down to Courmayeur.

4. *St. Barthélemy*

    This valley does not rise on the frontier ridge but is carried out of the great broad watershed between the Val Pelline and the Val Tournanche. The river enters the Dora Baltea at Nus.

5. *Val Tournanche*

    The Marmore drains the S flank of the Monte Cervino and flows straight S through Breuil, Valtournanche and Ante Saint André on the way down to Châtillon in the Aosta valley. The St. Théodule Pass at its head is one of the easiest of glacier passes in the Alps and consequently most frequented.

6. *Val d'Ayas*

    Two small streams flow from Plan Rosa and the Breithorn and unite at St. Jacques. The Evançon then flows in an elongated 'S' through Ayas, Brusson and Challand St. Anselme to Verres.

7. *Val di Gressoney*

    Carries the Lys from the Liskamm slopes on a very straight course S through the villages of Gressoney-la-Trinité and Gressoney-St.-Jean and Gaby to Pont St. Martin.

8. *Val Sesia*

    The longest valley draining the Pennine Alps, it turns this way and that in a generally south-east direction away from Monte Rosa. From Alagna Valsesia the Sesia flows through Riva,

Mollia and Scopello to Varallo and Borgosesia, picking up the Sermenza and the Mastallone streams from their long valleys draining the substantial eastern arm of the Monte Rosa 'star'.

9. *Valle Anzasca*

   With the resort of Macugnaga at its head, beneath the massive east wall of Monte Rosa, this short valley runs east to join the principal Valle d'Ossola at Piedmulera.

10. *Val di Antrona*

    With the next valley it is one of the north-easternmost valleys draining the edge of the Pennine Alps, with Villadóssola at its end.

11. *Valle di Bognanco*

    Carries the Cascata to Domodóssola.

Here the circuit leaves Italy and enters Switzerland. On this side the valleys, from E to W, are:

1. *The Saltine*

   Short and steep, leading down from the Simplon to Brig.

2. *The Nanztal*

   Carries the Gamsca northward to Brig.

3. *The Visptal*

   A short valley running up from Visp southwards to Stalden, where it splits to create the Saastal and the Mattertal.

4. *Saastal*

   Running down from the frontier watershed at Monte Moro through Saas Grund to Stalden.

5. *Mattertal*

   The most famous valley in Switzerland, descending from Zermatt, through Täsch, Randa and St. Niklaus to Stalden.

6. *Turtmantal*

   A short valley running straight to Turtmann and the Rhône, with Gruben its only village.

7. *Val d'Anniviers*

   The Navisence flows down the *Val de Zinal* to Ayer where the valley is re-named as it carries the river through Vissoie to Chippis and Sierre. A tributary side valley carries the Gougra down the *Val de Moiry* through Grimentz.

8. *Val d'Hérens*

   A substantial valley with a major side valley. From Arolla the Borgne is carried down to Les Hauderès, where the Ferpécle comes in from the E. The main valley continues through Evolène down to Sierre.

9. *Val d'Hérémence*

   Uniting with the former, this major branch of the Val d'Hérens carries the Dixence from the Val des Dix.

10. *Val de Nendaz*

    A short valley to the W of the Hérémence.

11. *Val de Bagnes*

    The Drance flows down from Mauvoisin through Fionnay to Sembrancher and Martigny. It is from the head of this valley that our expedition starts.

12. *Vallée d'Entremont*

    Carrying the other branch of the Drance from the Grand St. Bernard Pass through Liddes and Orsières to Sembrancher.

   In order to obtain a comprehensive picture of the whole of these Pennine Alps it is necessary to do a circuit of the Monte Rosa range, returning to one's starting point. One of the advantages of a circular tour is that you can start from any point on the circuit: I have recommended an anti-clockwise circuit as this is the finest way of approaching Monte Rosa - starting from Martigny, the easiest town of access, over the heads of all the valleys from the Valpelline to the Valle Anzasca, then returning over the spurs on the Swiss side from Saas Fee back to Verbier. As Hubert Walker suggested in his *Walking in the Alps*: *"there is experienced a gradual crescendo of scenic splendour, from mildness through grandeur to sheer overwhelming magnificence as the mighty cliffs of Monte Rosa are approached, encircled and finally breached."*

Of course, as there are so many passes over the ridges which separate one valley from the next, on both sides of the frontier, there is no single route. There are more than 80 passes which one could cross in making a circuit of Monte Rosa. Some are serious undertakings suitable only for experienced mountaineers, and they have been excluded from this guide. Some passes lead you down into valleys where onward continuation is inconvenient or necessitates a long road walk, and these passes have been excluded also. Nevertheless, some 50 routes and passes are described in this guide, making possible a number of combinations to create a circuit.

This Guide outlines the options of routes, the selection of which is entirely up to the individual. However, certain principles have governed my choice of routes so as to give the following guidance:

- take the best route from the scenic or aesthetic point of view;
- take the higher, rougher, least frequented, more interesting way;
- link up the greatest possible number of viewpoints by climbing adjacent peaks on the way;
- avoid the lower, easier and more popular routes;
- if a compromise is necessary because of the popular appeal of a beautiful place, then make the least popular approach;
- avoid as far as possible the main channels of tourist traffic and the main centres of tourist resort;
- elect to spend the night in little inns or alpine huts beyond the confines of a village rather than in the large hotels in a village.

The observance of these principles will ensure that you will get the most enjoyment out of your Grand Tour of Monte Rosa.

GENERAL INFORMATION

A. WHEN TO GO
The length of the alpine summer season is relatively short.

The earliest time to consider a walking tour in the Pennine Alps is June, but the snows may not have gone from the passes above 2500m until possibly the beginning of July. Late June/early July is the best time for the alpine flowers but these may only perhaps be found on the alpine pastures, the lower valley meadows having been mown by late spring/early summer. August is usually hot, but thunderstorms are not uncommon: even in summer a snowstorm above 2000m is not unusual, and can prevent some passes being crossed. Early September is probably the optimum period, with clear skies by day but cool at night. By mid-September nights can be cold and the first snows of winter arrive.

The Pennine Alps are generally the driest Alps, with less rainfall than the Bernese Oberland to the north and the Engadine to the east. Only a quarter of the annual precipitation falls in the summer months and then only an average of 10 days in each month. Half of those 30 days may be thundery.

If you are going high, or even only over the middle passes, you may be intending to stay at the alpine huts - club or private. As most of these are not accessible until the spring snows have gone they are usually only open from mid-June and they begin to close by mid-September. By late September/early October it will be difficult to find accommodation anywhere.

B. HOW TO GET THERE
Air
The most convenient airport is Geneva, but Lyons, Basle, Zurich, Turin and Milan may also be used, though they involve lengthy transfers by rail.

Direct and regular flights between the UK and Switzerland are operated by Swissair in conjunction with British Airways: London (Heathrow and Gatwick) and Manchester to Geneva. Other carriers (e.g. Air Lingus) from London (Gatwick) and other airports usually to Basle or Zurich.

Flight information may be obtained from Swissair, Swiss Centre, New Coventry Street, London W1V 4BJ (tel: 0171-439-4144) or from British Airways, 156 Regent Street, London W1R 5TA. (For all enquiries tel: 01345-222111).

Air services from North America fly from Atlanta, Boston, Chicago, Dallas, Detroit, Houston, Kansas, Los Angeles, Montreal, New York, San Francisco, Washington and other cities to Geneva and/or Zurich. Carriers are Air France (via Paris), British Airways (via Heathrow), Delta, KLM (via Amsterdam), Lufthansa (via Frankfurt), North West (via Amsterdam), Swissair, Trans World Airlines, United and Air Canada.

Rail

Rail is used for the transfer from Geneva airport - from the arrival hall concourse direct to the new (1989) station - then the international line via Lausanne, Montreux, Martigny, Sion, Sierre and Brig, and on to the Simplon and Domodóssola.

From Britain the rail journey to Switzerland is straightforward. The London - Paris - Dijon - Lausanne - Brig - Milan route uses the superfast TGV trains on some daytime services between Paris and Lausanne, but the overnight services on this route - the Simplon Express, Galilei and Rialto trains - arrive too early in the morning at Lausanne and Brig to be of any convenience. At Lausanne transfer to the Rhône valley line for stations as above.

The London - Florence - Venice - Paris - Culoz - Aix-les-Bains - Chamonix route uses TGV trains on daytime routes between Paris and Aix-les-Bains, while there is an overnight and sleeper service between Paris and St. Gervais. From Chamonix the SAT/SAVDA buses transfer through the Mont Blanc tunnel to Courmayeur and Aosta.

Rail travel on the Italian side of the Pennine Alps is less convenient. The Paris - Dijon - Chambéry - Modane - Turin - Rome route is useful for the Turin - Aosta connection: the Stendhal overnight and sleeper service is to be preferred to the Palatino service. From Turin Porta Nuova the Aosta service runs via Chiavasso to Ivrea, Verrés, St. Vincent and Châtillon for the Italian valleys.

Within Switzerland rail journeys are legendary. From Chamonix (France) to Martigny; from the Bernese Oberland via Kandersteg and the Lötschberg tunnel to Brig; from the Engadine on the *Glacier Express,* from St. Moritz to Zermatt via Chur and Brig; and from Domodóssola through the Simplon tunnel to Brig.

From Martigny the *MO Bahn* runs to Le Châble via Sembrancher while from Brig the *BVZ Bahn* runs through Visp and St. Niklaus to Zermatt.

Road

Fast toll-free autoroutes run from the Channel ports: E40/A10 Ostende, Bruxelles, A4/E25 through Luxembourg to Metz and Strasbourg. Here the E52 links to the E35 through Germany for entry into Switzerland at Basle. Alternatively, the A26 toll route from Calais runs across France via Reims, becoming the E50 'Autoroute de l'Est' to Metz and Strasbourg. On entry into Switzerland a special annual motorway tax is payable, enabling a fast drive on the N2, N1 and N6 via Bern and Montreux and then the N9 into the Rhône valley.

Alternatively there are fast autoroutes through France on the A6 'Autoroute du Soleil' to Mâcon, then the A40 to Geneva, continuing as the 'Autoroute Blanche' to the outskirts of Chamonix. Then take the Mont Blanc tunnel for Courmayeur and the S26 Aosta valley (or even the S27 road from Martigny over/under the Grand St. Bernard Pass to Aosta) for the Italian side of the Pennine Alps.

Local Public Transport

In some places in this Guide I have quoted actual times from the rail and bus timetables valid up to the end of May 1995. They give a useful indication of times of travel but though rail and bus timetables vary little between summer and winter, or from year to year, it is advisable that you check times locally. Timetables are available from rail and bus stations, post offices and tourist information offices.

C. CURRENCY

Until we can all walk about with Ecus in our pockets two currencies will be required for the GTMR - Swiss francs and Italian lire.

Swiss francs are available in notes of 100 (blue), 50 (green), 20 (blue) and 10 (red) francs and coins of 5, 2, 1, and $^1/_2$ francs and 20 and 10 centimes. The rate of exchange is about 2.0 SF per £1.00 sterling. Italian lire is available in notes of 100,000 (brown), 50,000 (purple), 10,000 (violet), 5000 (green) and 1000 (pink) lire and coins of 500, 200, 100, 50, 20 and 10 lire. The rate of exchange is about 2200 lire per £1.00 sterling.

Travellers cheques are useful but the opportunity to cash them will be limited to the main villages, bureaux de change/cambio at railway stations and tourist offices. Small denomination values will be useful where the rate of exchange at hotels might be unfavourable.

Major credit cards are more likely to be accepted for the purchase of goods or gifts than for services and are more widely acceptable in the Valais than in the Italian valleys.

Banks have strange hours of opening, but are more easily accessible for those having a day on the hills than in Britain, being open early in the mornings and in the early evenings.

Be prepared to pay cash at the high alpine huts for accommodation and meals and be considerate by not proffering notes of too high a denomination.

D. INSURANCE

Hopefully you will be able to complete your GTMR without mishap, but accidents and injuries do occur - a badly twisted ankle or being hit by dislodged stones are risks one has to face. Medical care and hospitalisation costs a lot of money, particularly in Switzerland. Ordinary holiday insurance may not cover persons engaged in mountaineering pursuits: check the small print!

Mountain rescue is **not** covered; special policies are available:

a) British Mountaineering Council, Crawford House, Precinct Centre, Booth Street East, Manchester M13 9RZ (tel: 0161-273- 5385) - available only to members of the BMC or to members of climbing clubs affiliated to the BMC.

b) West Mercia Insurance Services, High Street, Wombourne, nr Wolverhampton WV5 9DN (tel: 01902-892661).

Members of the Swiss Alpine Club are covered for mountain rescue/ helicopter rescue.

Personal or holiday insurance is essential for mountaineering trips, even in countries where under National Health Service arrangements reciprocal medical agreements are available for British citizens. The DSS publish two leaflets, *Protect Your Health Abroad* and *Medical Cover Abroad*. Copies can be obtained from the DSS Leaflets Unit, Box 20, Stanmore HA7 1AY. You will need to obtain Form E111 from your local DSS office or Post Office. Make a photocopy and take both copies with you.

E. THE LANGUAGE

The traveller on the GTMR will pass through three principal language zones - French, Italian and German - and a few areas of local dialect. The non-linguist may have difficulty in conversing with the locals met in the mountains - the cow-hands and shepherds, the chamois hunters, the woodsmen and other workmen - as very few speak English. It must be remembered that the high mountains and narrow valleys prevented much travel in the old days and so ensured the preservation of local customs and local dialects. Early settlers brought their own languages and in some parts the 'official' language is in the minority.

French is the language spoken in the Lower Valais - to the west of Sierre - and is also found in the valleys north of Aosta. Italian predominates between Breuil/Cervinia and the Simplon, while German is spoken in the three valleys running down to Brig.

The original Romance-speaking inhabitants of the Zermatt valley gave way in the 15thC to a German-speaking population from the Upper Valais - to the east of Sierre - though some of the old place-names still survive under a Teutonic veneer. On the other hand, about 1250, the Saas valley was colonised by Italian-speaking men from the Val Anzasca, while rather later some German-speaking inhabitants of the lower parts of the Saas valley settled at Macugnaga, the effect on the local names being an interesting parallel and contrast to what happened in the Zermatt valley. In the 13thC, too, a German-speaking colony settled at the head of the Val de Lys, probably brought there from over the Théodule Pass by the lord of that territory, the Bishop of Sion. It was probably this colony which sent out offshoots to Alagna and Rima, though possibly these are due to the energies of the Counts of Biandrate, who were the promoters of the Saas and Macugnaga colonies. The historical importance of the Théodule and the Monte Moro passes (and also the glacier routes over minor passes, such as that from Saas to the Antrona valley) are significant to the settlement and language of this region of the Pennine Alps.

English may well be understood in most of the villages in Switzerland, particularly in hotels and restaurants, but less likely in the Italian valleys. It will be a distinct help to have some acquaintance with the spoken and written language of the area as in some places enquiries as to directions and accommodation may only be possible with some people in their own language.

A glossary of map and mountain terms in the principal languages is given in Appendix B.

F. PREPARATION AND PRECAUTIONS

Crossing the many ridges and valleys that radiate outwards from the Monte Rosa watershed means crossing the grain of the country: up and down steep valley sides, through dark thick forests and over rocky passes. Your first pass should be as enjoyable as your last: the first few days on the GTMR will be an ordeal unless you are properly prepared. The fitter you are the more you will enjoy your Tour.

It helps to be in good physical condition. Daily you will be walking at altitudes between 1400m and 3300m (4500ft - 11,000ft), climbing sometimes very steep slopes and needing 2-3hrs to ascend to the pass. You should be able to walk at a leisurely pace and without discomfort and manage 300m (1000ft) vertical per hour.

To prepare for the walk you should be able to

- fellwalk 400 vertical metres per hour (1300ft) or
  4km (2.5mls) distance per hour on a regular basis, or
- run 8km (5mls) in 45min. 3 times a week for 3 months at least.

But the best preparation is fell walking itself, wearing your boots and carrying a 10kg (22lb) rucksack.

It is no good expecting that the walk itself will get you fit. If you are not in good shape the first 3-5 days may be miserable for you: soft skin on the feet will produce blisters if you have not worn boots regularly. If your shoulders are unaccustomed to carrying a rucksack swollen tendons on the clavicle can become uncomfortable.

Those living in the hills and mountains will be better acclimatised than those living at sea level. A person in good physical condition usually acclimatises better than one who is in poor condition. Good physical condition = strength and endurance. Proper acclimatisation = the time required at altitude for your body to produce more red blood cells to carry more oxygen to the muscles. At 3000m (10,000 ft) there is 30% less oxygen in the air than at sea level.

Apart from aching lungs and muscles another discomfort will come from the sun. Ultra-violet rays can penetrate thin cloud layers and at altitude sunburn can be quite severe. Protect your head, back of the neck, the shoulders and, if wearing shorts or skirts, the calf muscles and the sock-line.

G. MOUNTAIN SAFETY

Accidents can happen even to the fittest. If you are injured in Switzerland and need assistance and have to be rescued you will be charged for the service unless you are a member of the Swiss Alpine

Club or otherwise insured. Swiss Air Rescue can be called out by telephoning 01/383-11-11, but should only be used if absolutely essential.

In order to call assistance the alpine distress signal is universally recognised: six signals spaced evenly in one minute, then a minute pause, then six more signals, repeated for as long as necessary. The reply to the distress signal is a series of three signals spaced evenly in one minute repeated after a minute's pause. If your distress call is answered do not stop signalling: the rescuer will need to be guided to you, especially if there is poor visibility or if you lie hidden behind rocks. The signals may be visual or audible - your torch and whistle are carried for such emergencies.

H. CLOTHING AND EQUIPMENT

A good pair of comfortable, vibram-soled boots is essential; they will take much punishment on rock, scree and snow. Don't wear a pair that is too lightweight. A good maxim is that the heavier the rucksack you carry the heavier the boots should be. But don't carry too heavy a sack - 10kg (22lb) should be the maximum.

Enough has been said elsewhere about the three layer principle in clothing and there should be no need to repeat that advice here.

A good rucksack is essential. One with a capacity of 65 litres should be big enough to carry all your essential kit. Don't over-burden yourself with non-essentials. Take the following:

- dry undershirt and socks
- sweater (wool or fleece)
- good lightweight rainsuit for wet days
- sun hat and sun creams for sunny days
- mittens and ski hat (wool or fleece) for cold days
- thermos or 1 litre water bottle
- the usual safety equipment - map, compass, whistle, small torch and first aid kit essential. Altimeter useful
- first aid kit to include lip salve and items for blisters, cuts and grazes, and sunburn

- toilet kit. Soap is a necessity: it is not provided everywhere. Universal bath plug useful
- camping stove useful for boiling water for tea, coffee or soup
- sheet sleeping bag for use with blankets in huts
- lightweight slippers or shoes to wear inside huts: you can't always guarantee that there will be a supply of slippers in the hut. Your feet will need a rest from wearing boots all day
- change of clothes or track suit for use in hut/travelling

Ice axe, crampons and rope are not necessary, except if crossing glaciers, snowfields and passes early in the season. Instep crampons and collapsible spiked walking sticks are useful aids for the summer walker on the GTMR.

I. PATHS AND WAYMARKS

Footpaths are signposted and maintained by the Swiss and Italian Alpine Clubs, the local commune (in Italy) and in Switzerland the cantonal branches of the Swiss Footpath Protection Association (Schweizerische Arbeitegemeinschaft für Wanderwege). In addition, there are thousands of other paths and tracks, to remote alpine farms and pastures, and hunters and forestry paths.

Of the officially-maintained paths in Switzerland there are two types: Wanderweg and Bergweg. Wanderweg are the lower, valley paths, signposted with yellow markings. Bergweg are signposted with red and white markings and are usually those above the treeline. None of the main marked routes is dangerous. In the Italian Pennine Alps not all mountain footpaths are signposted.

Signposts usually indicate the height of their location and the places and their height on the routes indicated. They list walking time estimates in hours and minutes. The German *Stunde,* hour, is abbreviated St. Minutes are abbreviated Min. (= *minuten*). These times are about what the average walker will require for the journey

- actual walking time, exclusive of stops for rest, photography, etc.

Throughout this Guide I shall refer to these times as GBT = Guide Book Time. The times are a useful indicator of your fitness: don't be surprised to find in the first few days that they seem over-optimistic. By the second half of your tour, when you have become acclimatised, you will be able to do better than GBT. Remember the times are only averages.

Where paths are waymarked they will be with red and white flashes if Bergwegs, but you may find other markings in blue or yellow in different areas, or letters or numbers painted on rocks. These waymarks are usually for local walks, such as the Tour of the Combins in the Val des Bagnes (seen on Sections 1 and 2) or 'GB' for Gran Balconata in the Val Tournanche (seen on Sections 3 and 4). Numbered paths are those usually featured in local parish walking routes promoted by the tourist associations.

In some places the path may not be obvious, there may be no waymarks and the passes and destinations may not be signposted. Don't worry - this book gives detailed guidance.

Glaciers can be the most dangerous places and care must be taken, but the two most likely to be crossed - the Glacier de Cheilon between the Pas de Chèvres and the Dix hut (Section 13.1 - Volume 2) and the Grand Desert between the Cabane de Prafleuri and the Col de Louvie (Section 14.1 - Volume 2) are usually safe. Fresh snow may cover crevasses and there may be gaps at the edges, where the ice of the glacier meets the solid ground of the lateral moraine. Routes across these glaciers are marked by old ski sticks, poles with flags or painted rocks.

J. ACCOMMODATION

There is a wide variety of accommodation available in the valleys of the Pennine Alps - campsites, hotels, inns, *pensions* and *gasthofs*. Some of these advertise *dortoirs* or *matratzenlagers* - dormitory-style sleeping - in an attic or outbuilding, with bedding, washing and toilet facilities - at very reasonable prices.

There are other useful accommodations in the upper valleys - chalets, farms and even ski lift stations and restaurants may have a *dortoir* - and also the mountain huts - *refuges, cabanes* or *rifugi*.

Appendix A lists useful places of accommodation on the GTMR but inclusion is not necessarily a recommendation of its services.

Parties of three or more are advised to make reservations by telephone a day or two in advance - especially important in the height of the season - but the disadvantage with this arrangement is that you are tied to making a particular landfall each day: a neatly-planned arrangement can be thrown to the wind if you have to turn back before a pass is crossed, if you have an 'off-day' or if you have to outreach your capabilities to reach the hut before supper time. The need to sit out bad weather or take a rest day requires a flexible arrangement. If you know you cannot reach your pre-booked bed try to telephone to cancel it: this is especially important if you are staying at mountain huts - not only will the guardian needlessly call out the mountain rescue service to search for you but (s)he can allocate beds to others and cater accordingly. Also bear in mind that even though you may have booked your hut accommodation your reservation may not be held if you make an extremely late arrival.

Mountain Refuges

The existence and availability of mountain refuges is often a mystique to newcomers to the Alps, but there is no formality: they are open to anyone, but membership of an alpine club confers advantages such as priority of bed booking and reduction in overnight charges. (Membership of the UK Branch of the Austria Alpine Club provides these benefits for UK and overseas members. Write to the AAC at Box 43, Welwyn Garden City, Herts. AL8 6PQ. Alternatively write to the BMC (see under Insurance) for a reciprocal rights card if you are a BMC member). The expense of membership can only be recouped by staying at huts every night on a two-week tour and is hardly justifiable for an occasional user. Alpine club membership confers no advantages in private huts.

If you can afford to be flexible the best arrangement is to proceed as far as you feel able each day, aiming to arrive at your intended accommodation by late afternoon. Try to arrive after the day visitors have left: arriving early is the best way to guarantee a place, but not too early or the guardian may try to move you on to the next hut, which may be too far for you after the day's exertions.

On arrival at the hut remove your boots before entering and leave them in the space provided, usually just inside the front door. Help yourself to the hut slippers, if provided. Seek out the guardian to book your bed for the night and order any meals you may require: sometimes evening meals have to be ordered by 5pm, usually no later than 6pm. Mealtimes are usually displayed: if in doubt, ask.

Sometimes the guardian allocates you a specific bed - particularly if the hut is known to be filled - sometimes just the room, where you can help yourself to a bedspace. At the alpine huts mixed dormitory accommodation is provided, offering either bunk beds, mattresses on the floor or purpose-built sleeping platforms. Bedding consists of a pillow and two blankets: for hygiene reasons you may wish to provide your own sheet sleeping bag. Lay claim to your bedspace and make your bed while it is still light: many huts do not have illumination in the bedrooms.

Washing facilities are either non-existent or basic, and what there are are usually communal. There may be hot showers, or it may be a basin on the landing or a pipe and trough outside.

The evening meal is usually a set meal, served at about 7.30pm, and it is usually substantial, sufficient to cater for mountain appetites - soup, green salad, then a main course served with either rice or potatoes. There is sometimes a sweet course. Coffee and drinks are extra. The so-called continental breakfast is usually meagre and most experienced tourers supplement it with, or provide, their own. Hot water is available from the kitchen in jugs for you to make your own tea and fill your flasks: you may, or may not, be charged for it. (In village hotels breakfast has to be ordered as an extra and when it is provided it may not be available until 8am).

At mountain huts hand in your alpine club membership card (passports in hotels) and complete a registration document. Settle your bill before retiring to bed and collect your card/passport at the same time: the hut guardian will be too busy getting breakfasts ready in the morning, while in hotels only a waitress may be on duty.

The mountain huts are primarily for the use of climbers who need to make very early (pre-dawn) starts for their alpine routes. The guardian may ask you if you wish to rise at 4.30am or 7am and allocate you a room accordingly. Otherwise be prepared to be disturbed by those rising and leaving early: conversely, do not disturb others if you go to bed after the early-risers. In many huts the generator is turned off at 10pm.

K. FLORA AND FAUNA

The valleys of the Pennine Alps are thickly wooded and the treeline extends up to c2000m (6500ft). Up to about 1000m (3300ft) are mixed hardwoods of ash, beech, lime, oak and sycamore. The uppermost limit of oak is c1000m (3300ft), with beech up to c1300m (4300ft). Above this level and up to the treeline are the coniferous trees - larch *Larix decidua,* silver fir *Abies alba,* with Norway spruce *Picea abies,* the dominant species up to c1800m (6000ft), while above these grow the Scots pine *Pinus sylvestris.* The upper limit is marked by the mountain pine *Pinus mugo,* and the Arolla or stone pine *Pinus cembra.* Ground cover shrubs such as the juniper *Juniperus communis* grow up to the Scots pine level while Alpine bilberry *Vaccinium gaultherioides* and rust-leaved alpenrose *Rhododendron ferrugineum* grow in the Arolla pine belt.

The snowline lies from 600-100m (2000-3500ft) above the treeline and the zone between is the area of high alpine pastures, where cattle and sheep graze in summer. The rocks of the Pennine Alps are mostly silicaceous and mainly poor in calcium and the soils are mostly acidic, but on these alpine pastures there is an abundance of nitrogen as a by-product of grazing animals. As a consequence these high meadows are the habitat for more than 700 species of rich and varied flowers, seen at their best in late June/early July.

A number of these alpine plants are endangered or vulnerable species and are protected by nature conservancy regulations and other measures. Flower-picking and digging out is prohibited in many areas: Post Offices, tourist information offices, hotels and the alpine refuges display posters indicating those varieties protected by law. A tour of the GTMR will be enhanced by a knowledge and appreciation of the flowers that will be seen. The Swiss Alpine Club's pocket-book *Our Alpine Flora* is invaluable: it is about the size of this guidebook and since 1989 has been available in an English edition (ISBN 3-85902-098-6).

Of wildlife, the chamois *Rupicapra rupicapra* and Alpine marmot *Marmota marmota* are common above the treeline, the latter more often heard than seen, its shrill call on the bouldery slopes of the upper meadows warning others to take cover. Less common is the big-horned Alpine ibex *Capra ibex* but herds may be seen near the Monte Moro and Col de Louvie, and at other high altitudes.

The raven *Corvus corax* and Alpine swift *Apus melba* are common above the treeline, while the Alpine chough *Pyrrhocorax graculus* fancies rocky places on the ridges of the mountains: as soon as you sit down on a pass or peak to eat your lunch scavenging choughs are bound to appear. Buzzards *Buteo buteo* are the most likely large bird of prey to be seen. Wheatear *Oenanthe oenanthe,* stonechat *Saxicola torquata,* black redstart *Phoenicurus ochruros,* and Blue Rock Thrush *Monticola solitarius* are found on the rocky slopes and high alpine pastures, while the brown/black, white-spotted, fast-flying, raucous jay-like bird seen and heard in the treeline is the nutcracker *Nucifraga caryocatactes,* which feeds on the seeds of the Arolla pine.

L. MAPS

The Swiss Federal Topographic Service (Eidgennersiche Landestopographie) publish the official Carte Nationale de la Suisse or Landeskerten der Schweiz (LS) maps, which cover the whole of the area traversed by the GTMR. They are of excellent quality and detail.

For general planning the following sheets of the 1:100,000 scale

Bagnes and 47, Monte Rosa. Only small parts of Sheets 41 and 42 cover the northernmost Swiss Valais. Sheets 46 and 47 include all of Sections 1-8 and 14 of this Guide, and most of Section 13. Sheet 42 covers Sections 9 and 10. These sheets are in red covers.

Seven sheets of the 1:50,000 scale cover all of the GTMR. Though they do not have a notation of conventional signs they have grid lines at 1km intervals, contours at 20m intervals and hill shading, which make them easy to read and use. These sheets are in green covers:

273	Montana	parts of Sections 11 and 12
274	Visp	Sections 9 and 10
282	Martigny	parts of Sections 1 and 14
283	Arolla	parts of Sections 1, 2 and 14, and Section 13
284	Mischabel	part of Section 7, and Section 8
293	Valpelline	parts of Sections 2 and 4, and Section 3
294	Gressoney	parts of Sections 4 and 7, and Sections 5 and 6

LS have published two special 1:50,000 scale sheets in yellow covers which cover substantial parts of the GTMR in the Valais. They are called 'Walkers Maps' (Carte Pédestre/Wanderkarte) and show footpaths, alpine refuges, PTT bus routes and bus stops over-printed in red. They are Sheets 283 Arolla and 5006 Zermatt-Saas Fee. Sheet 5006 is a composite of Sheets 284, the eastern half of 283 and the southern halves of 273 and 274.

IGC of Turin - the Central Geographical Institute - publish a series of maps at 1:50,000 scale, two of which cover a large part of the route. Sheet 5, Cervino-Matterhorn and Monte Rosa covers Sections 2-6 inclusive, while Sheet 10, Monte Rosa, Alagna and Macugnaga covers Sections 6 to 8 inclusive.

The publishers Kompass also do two maps at 1:50,000 scale. Sheet 87, Breuil/Cervinia-Zermatt covers Sections 2-5 and Sheet 88, Monte Rosa covers Sections 6-8.

Though neither IGC nor Kompass are necessarily as accurate or detailed as the LS maps they do show paths and path numbers and alpine refuges over-printed in red.

Studio FMB of Bologna also do tourist maps with paths, path numbers and alpine refuges. Their walking maps at 1:50,000 scale (under the name 'Eurocart') have no sheet numbers but their title Cervino/Monte Rosa covers most of Sections 3 to 6.

The greater detail of 1:25,000 scale maps is not really required for the GTMR: in any case, a lot of sheets would be needed to cover the route. IGC's Sheets 108 Cervino/Breuil/Champoluc and 109 Monte Rosa/Alagna/Macugnaga/Gressoney cover most of Sections 4-7 but the unreliability of the routes of some paths shown casts doubt upon the accuracy of the others. With the exception of the LS maps, most of the 1:25,000 scale maps are just enlargements of the 1:50,000 scale: they don't necessarily show more information, but are easier to read.

Tourist information offices in the main resorts publish their own footpaths maps: some are very sketchy and free, while those in the Valais are usually special edition LS maps at 1:50,000 or 1:25,000 scales, and pricey.

Maps and Map Profiles in this Guide

There is usually a choice of routes from one valley to the next and a key map is given at the start of each section. The maps for each route are based on the 1:50,000 scale, but they are reduced to fit the size of the page. The horizontal scales of each map are the same, and they are orientated so that true north is at the top of the page, unless otherwise indicated.

The profiles indicate the relative steepness of the ground. Heights marked on profiles correspond to the heights marked on the maps.

Be careful in attempting to translate distance into walking time. The state of the path, steepness, altitude, terrain, etc. may require different walking times for routes that appear to have similar profiles. An attempt has been made in the text to give an average time from point to point - the GBT (Guide Book Time).

Mont Velan, 3731m, from the Col de Montagnaya, 2899m (Section 3)

The Cabane de Chanrion, 2462m, Val de Bagnes
Chateau des Dames, 3488m, from the Col de Valcournera, 3066m

M. USING THIS GUIDE

The GTMR is described in fourteen sections, each relating to the principal valley systems and, coincidentally, a section for each day of a two-week tour. Each section has an introduction describing the characteristics of the section between one valley and the next and indicates, from the frontier watershed radiating outwards towards the lower valleys, the passes between those valleys. These passes are described in sub-sections to each main section, or chapter.

Some of the passes are easier than others, and some are more interesting than others. Some are long and steep, some are short but do not involve much ascent/descent, and the converse also applies: long and low, and short and steep. Some passes enjoy superb views, others none, and some have conveniently accessible adjoining peaks having commanding panoramas. There are some passes that are outside the scope of this guide because of their degree of difficulty.

It may not be easy therefore, for the first-time visitor to the Pennine Alps, to decide which pass to cross from one valley to the other. Which route is going to pass through the finest mountain scenery and have continuous interest throughout? This must be the principal criterion for selecting your route on the GTMR and I have therefore rated each option with a grade and star system. This is a somewhat subjective assessment, but it provides a useful guide to enable comparisons to be made between different routes.

The difficulty of the terrain is graded from 1 (easiest) to 5 (hardest):

1	Easy	4	Rough
2	Good	5	Tough
3	Reasonable		

The quality of the routes is indicated by stars, with three stars indicating the best. The lack of stars does not necessarily mean that the pass is not worth crossing.

Distances and heights given in this Guide are metric. Horizontal distances are given in kilometres (quoted km) or metres (quoted metres). Vertical distances are also in metres, but quoted m, after height, e.g. 2394m.

Times are expressed in hours (hr) and minutes (min. to distinguish from m for metres). Times are approximate: they are averages for an alpinist or fit, regular walker.

Directions 'right' and 'left' apply to the direction of travel, whether in ascent, descent or traverse, but when applied to glaciers, streams or rivers is the direction of flow.

All the routes described are based on personal survey and were correct at the time of the guidebook going to print, but any corrections required to keep the guide up-to-date will be made in future editions where possible. The author would welcome information on any changes that are necessary. Please write to me c/o Cicerone Press.

*Looking down the Comba di Vessona from L'Ardamun, 2206m. (Section 3)
The Col du Crête Sèche, 2899m, is the lowest point on the skyline across the
Val Pelline*

SECTION 1
MARTIGNY and the VAL de BAGNES

Our circuit of the GTMR starts at Le Châble in the Val de Bagnes, but to get there it is usual to start from Martigny. By using car, post bus or train you can get a long way up the valley before the walk proper begins, at the Lac de Mauvoisin. By car or by post bus you can get as far as Mauvoisin, 35km from Martigny (but no further than Lourtier in winter). The trains run as far as Le Châble, where you can transfer to the post bus.

At Martigny railway station trains of the *MO Bahn* depart from Platform MO, next to Platform 1:

Train No.	108	120	122
Martigny dep	08.58	13.55	15.36
Le Châble arr	09.27	14.24	16.04

There are several other trains from Martigny to Le Châble (from 07.14 to 19.55) but these are the only ones that have connections with the post bus from Le Châble to Mauvoisin. Relevant buses are:

Service No.	71070	71150	71170
Le Châble dep	09.30	14.30	16.20
Mauvoisin arr	10.15	15.15	17.05

(but only between 25 June and 25 September).

There are other post buses from Le Châble, but they only go as far as Lourtier, from where there is a long (3hr 30min.) road walk up to Mauvoisin. From Mauvoisin there is a 3hr walk up to the hut at Chanrion.

Whether by train or by road, by post bus, car or on foot, our journey starts at Martigny and goes up the Val de Bagnes. From Martigny the road crosses the Drance and follows it at first S then in an E direction as it winds beneath the base of Le Catogne, 2598m. It then crosses the river again at Bovernier and proceeds through a wild and narrow defile, passing at one point through a tunnel about 60m/200ft long. This part of the valley still shows traces of the terrible floods of 1818.

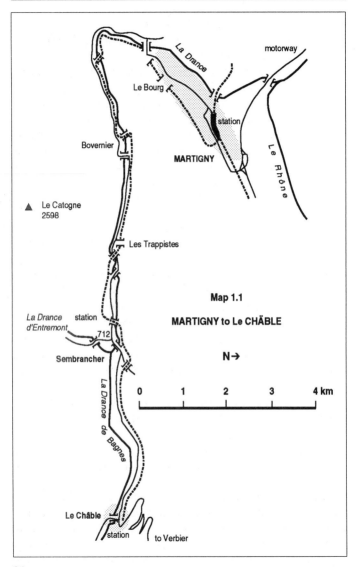

Map 1.1

MARTIGNY to Le CHÂBLE

N→

Immediately beyond the tunnel the railway, then the road, cross the river again at a place called Les Trappistes, recalling the remains of a convent which was inhabited by Trappist monks in 1797, but originally a building connected with some abandoned iron mines, which were destroyed by that flood.

Just after this you reach Sembrancher, 712m (14km/9mls from Martigny), standing at the meeting of the two branches of the Drance - that flowing from the Grand St. Bernard down the Val d'Entremont and that flowing from the Val de Bagnes. Sembrancher was the birthplace in 1742 of Monsieur J.L.Murith, later (1792-1816) Prior of the Grand St. Bernard monastery, a celebrated botanist and the first to climb Mont Velan, in 1779. The Val d'Entremont leading to the Grand St. Bernard pass and Aosta has from very early times been one of the main channels of communication across the Alps. The pass was used by the Romans under Constantine the Younger and by Napoleon, and was annually crossed by hundreds of pilgrims. The celebrated Hospice was one of the earliest, if not the earliest, of its kind. It was founded in the 9thC, but in Bourg St. Pierre then transferred and refounded in the 11thC on the crest of the pass by St. Bernard of Menthon (above the Lake of Annecy).

But the scenery of the Grand St. Bernard is dull and uninteresting, contrasting with the parallel pass through the Val de Bagnes and over the Col de Fenêtre, which had been familiar to the natives for many centuries. The Val de Bagnes only became known to the outside world by the destructive flood which in 1818 issued from its narrow mouth to carry destruction even beyond Martigny, and later, in the 1840s and 1850s by indefatigable mountaineers such as Professor James Forbes, Herren Bernhard Studer (1794-1887, Professor of Geology at Berne) and Melchior Ulrich, closely followed by Mr. W. Mathews.

The Val de Bagnes was under the rule of the Abbots of St. Maurice until the conquest of the Lower Valais by the Upper Valais in 1475, the bridge below Mauvoisin (sometimes called the Pont de Quart) marking the limit between their jurisdiction and that of the lordships of Quart, in the valley of Aosta. In former times the valley was

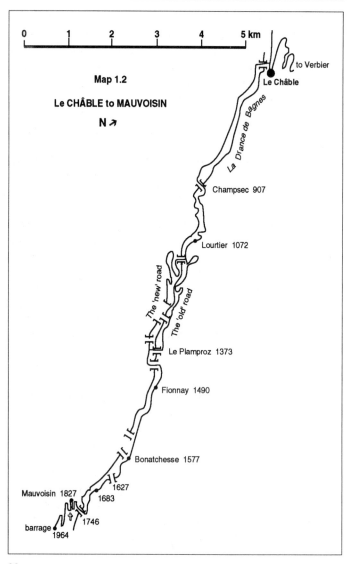

celebrated for its mineral springs and baths from which it is named.

Six km/3.5mls from Sembrancher on the R bank of the Drance de Bagnes is Le Châble, 821m, the main village of the valley. It is at the end of the railway line from Martigny and is the place where you leave the valley for the ski resort of Verbier high up above. The Abbey of Le Châble was formerly the summer residence of the Abbot of St. Maurice.

We can return to this place at the end of our Grand Tour of Monte Rosa with a descent from Verbier.

Le Châble is the last village in the Val de Bagnes from where you can buy supplies: there are none available at Lourtier or Fionnay. Buy food for lunch today and for breakfast and lunch tomorrow. The next supplies are at Ollomont and Valpelline, but not Bionaz. There are bars and telephones at Lourtier and Fionnay and a restaurant and telephone at Mauvoisin. Accommodation is available at Lourtier, Fionnay, Mauvoisin and at the head of the valley in the Swiss Alpine Club's Chanrion hut. (See Appendix A).

You are most likely to start walking from the road head at Mauvoisin, but should you be walking from lower down the valley, having missed that vital post bus, or needing an early leg stretch, the following information and walking times will apply:

Map: **LS 1:50,000   282 Martigny and 283 Arolla**
Distance: **10km from Mauvoisin Barrage**
                              (16km from Fionnay, 26km from Le Châble)
Height Gain: **498m by W bank or 678m by E bank**
Height Loss: **Nil by W bank, 142 by E bank**

Outward		G.B.T.	Return	
		Le Châble, 821m	**6hr 15**	**1hr**
1hr 15	**1hr 15**	**Lourtier, 1072m**	**5hr 15**	**1hr 15**
1hr 30	**2hr 45**	**Fionnay, 1490m**	**4hr**	**1hr 30**
1hr 30	**4hr 15**	**Mauvoisin, 1824m**	**2hr 30**	**2hr 30**
3hr	**7hr 15**	**Chanrion Hut, 2462m**		

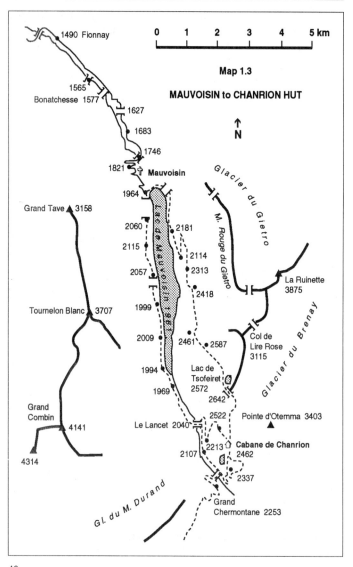

0   1   2   3   4   5 km

Map 1.3

MAUVOISIN to CHANRION HUT

↑
N

1490 Fionnay

1565
Bonatchesse 1577

1627

1683

1746

1821

† Mauvoisin

1964

Lac de Mauvoisin 1961

Grand Tave ▲ 3158

2060   2181

2115   2114

2057   2313

              2418

M. Rouge du Gietro

Glacier du Gietro

La Ruinette
3875

Tournelon Blanc ▲ 3707

1999

2009   2461 2587

Col de
Lire Rose
3115

Glacier du Brenay

1994

1969   Lac de
             Tsofeiret
             2572

             2642

Grand
Combin   4141

Pointe d'Otemma 3403 ▲

2522

Le Lancet 2040

4314

2213   † Cabane de Chanrion
2107   2462

            2337

Gl. du M. Durand

Grand
Chermontane 2253

The road crosses the Drance by a fine stone bridge and passes over a plain littered with boulders and debris to reach the hamlet of Champsec, 907m. It recrosses the Drance and winds up the hillside to the village of Lourtier, 1072m.

Above Lourtier both 'old' and 'new' roads mount by a series of zig-zags, but on opposite sides of the river which here, charged with the drainage of ten extensive glaciers, forces its way through a very narrow gorge.

The scenery is wild and picturesque, especially the little basin just before Le Plampraz, where the considerable stream from the Corbassière glacier joins the Drance. A short way beyond another green basin is reached and a bridge is crossed to Fionnay, 1490m, (29km/18mls from Martigny), beautifully situated amongst fine woods. Apart from the Mauvoisin Hotel and the Chanrion Hut farther up the valley, the village is the last place for accommodation in the valley. It has an hotel, a pension and two dortoirs, and a tourist office.

Beyond Fionnay the scenery becomes wilder and wilder, the precipices of the Mont Pleurer, 3703m, towering on the L above. The road keeps to the R bank of the torrent, past the Bonatchesse huts, 1577m. Here a half-wooded rocky threshold separates the area of the mayens from that of the pastures. On these limestone rocks on the R bank of the river is to be found a rare saxifrage - *Saxifraga diapensoïdes* - restricted in Switzerland to the valleys of the Bagnes, Entremont and Zermatt.

The 'old' road crossed the torrent by the solid stone bridge called Pont de Mauvoisin (or Pont de Quart), where the Drance is channelled into a narrow gorge. The bridge was rebuilt in 1828 some 30m above the waters after the disastrous flood of 1818 had carried away the earlier one.

The modern road is much higher than the old road and zig-zags up to the Mauvoisin Hotel, 1824m, perched on a hillock or spur, while there is a little chapel just beyond. The terrace at Mauvoisin is very attractive with its larches. Botanists used to come here in search of an alpine form of birch (*Betula Murithii* - named after the prior of the St. Bernard Hospice) and the Tansy-leaved rocket, *Hugueninia*

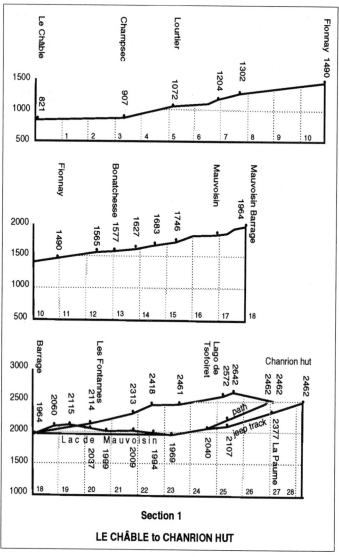

Section 1

LE CHÂBLE to CHANRION HUT

Forbes came into the Val de Bagnes in August 1842 on an excursion into the Pennine Alps, having already completed his own Tour of Mont Blanc. Commenting on the devastating force of the torrent when the Drance flooded twenty-four years earlier, he wrote:

"...the river is discharged through a sort of chasm, which shows evident marks (of the flood). The character of the scenery becomes more grand, the walnut trees and irrigation disappear, and we are once more in the region of pines and savage rocks. We remarked here a pretty illustration of the friction of glaciers as distinguished from that of water. The side of one of the ravines through which the stream struggles is distinctly marked on its bold limestone surface by the long grooves which have been considered peculiarly characteristic of the abrasion of glaciers. Though the descent is very steep, and the wall of the rock almost vertical, these chiselled and polished grooves are worn out in a nearly horizontal, slightly declining direction, and are continuous for many yards or fathoms. Superimposed upon these, on the very same surface, are the marks of wear resulting from the action of floods, probably charged with great masses of debris. The water marks are rough and contused, quite in contrast with the smooth prolongation of the other. They also slope downwards at an angle similar to that of the river bed, whilst, as has been said, the others are nearly horizontal."

Tanacetifolia, found in Switzerland only in the valleys of the Drance and Hérens.

The rustic hotel was built in 1863, in the wake of the early explorers of the valley. The rectangular chapel, with a circular apse and domed roof, was reconstructed in 1730 on the site of a 13thC fortified tower.

Held high above the Val de Bagnes on its E side is a vast field of névé, the Gietro Glacier, that is not visible from below. Its outlet is through a narrow channel on the S flank of Le Pleureur, discharging into the valley above Mauvoisin and the cause of several catastrophes as masses of ice broke off and fell down a steep rock wall to block the narrow valley.

In 1595 glacial debris descended into the valley and formed a barrier behind which the waters of the Drance accumulated until they burst through, on 4 June, and swept through the valley below, carrying off 110 people and many cattle and houses.

In the spring of 1818 the glacier again choked the valley in a similar fashion forming a dam nearly 90m/300ft high, behind which the Drance soon formed a lake nearly 1km/1.5mls in length and very deep. A recurrence of the former catastrophe seemed inevitable, but an eminent engineer of the Valais, Herr Venetz, undertook to avert it by driving a tunnel through the ice barrier. Gangs of men worked day and night for 34 days between 10 May and 13 June digging a tunnel through the ice and debris completing it just as the waters of the lake reached the level of the tunnel. The flow of water rapidly enlarged and lowered the opening and in less than three days 40% of the water had safely run off into the river's customary channel. In the meantime, however, the dam of ice and debris had been weakened by the excavating action of the outflow, and on 16 June 1818 it suddenly gave way. In half an hour a quantity of water five times greater than that of the Rhine at Basle - where it carries down the drainage of nearly the whole of the Swiss Alps - rushed through the breach and down the narrow valley. The flood spread destruction far and wide: blocks of stone, trees, houses and debris were carried into the valley of the Rhône well beyond Martigny. Although most of the inhabitants of the valley had been evacuated to safety beforehand some 34 people were carried away, along with 400 houses, all the bridges over the Drance and large numbers of cattle. The waters even reached the first floor level of the houses in Martigny. More permanent mischief was done by the masses of stone and gravel that were spread over the meadows in the lower levels of the valley, even below Martigny.

The impending danger of a renewal of the same catastrophe has since 1818 been averted by a simple and ingenious device, originated by Herr Venetz. A stream of water, at a temperature even but a little above freezing point, acts as a saw, which rapidly cuts through the glacier ice. The streams from the mountains are thus conducted in wooden troughs onto the accumulated masses of ice and frozen snow and thereby cut up into huge blocks, which fall into the Drance and are soon carried away and melted by the current. Men were later often employed in summer to conduct this operation, but the glacier has now shrunk, and but a small talus, formed by the ice avalanches from the snout of the glacier, some 600m/2000ft above, marks the site of the catastrophe of 1818.

There were two more floods: one in 1894 and another in 1898. That on 28 June 1894 was the more terrible, but not as bad as that of 1818. Seventeen bridges were destroyed and the flood nearly broke through the dykes at Martigny. It rushed down in 5hrs from Chermontane to Martigny, but no houses were ruined, nor was there any loss of life of man or beast. It originated in a small lake formed at the foot of the Crête Sèche glacier, near its junction with the Otemma glacier. The high moraine on the L bank of the later glacier and the ice stream itself blocked the waters which generally flowed out through subglacial channels, then choked also. The dammed up water succeeded in finding an issue through a crevasse, and rapidly enlarging this aperture, dashed down into the valley.

The Barrage de Mauvoisin, 1964m, was constructed between 1951-58 to control the floodwaters of the Drance and to produce hydro-electric power. Were the Gietro glacier to advance again the blocks of ice would fall into the lake, there to be dissolved. The curving concrete dam is 235m high and 535m long and when full, at a level of 1960m, retains 177 million m^3, with a surface area of 205ha.

In winter 595 million kW are produced, and in summer 166 million kW.

At the Barrage a big horizon opens up - the huge Grand Combin to the SW and Mont Blanc de Cheilon to the SE, while behind, to the NE, is a striking view of Mont Pleurer.

It is at the Barrage de Mauvoisin that the real walking begins. There are two routes from here up to Chermontane and the Chanrion Hut:

      Option 1: that on the W bank (L)   Grade 1

      Option 2: that on the E bank (R)   Grade 2*

Both routes take about 3hr, but that above the E bank is the more interesting of the two, avoids a dull jeep track, and does not entail a final climb to the hut.

Option 1

From the W end of the Barrage a tunnel (illuminated) carries a motorable track through the cliff (max. height for vehicles is 1.6m), climbs to a height of 2115m and for a distance of c5km runs fairly level or descending (until opposite the moraine of the Brenay Glacier, the glacier itself having greatly shrunk). The track, created when the dam was constructed, passes opposite the waterfall from the Gietro glacier but this, and several minor glaciers on either side of the valley, are not seen from the track, but a glimpse is gained of the fine icefield of La Tsessette descending from a hollow N of the Tour de Boussine, 3833m, a great buttress of the Grand Combin, here rising above the valley in formidable precipices of black rock.

The road is rough but motorable for cars, though exposed to stonefall throughout the year and bad avalanches in winter. At the S end of the lake there is limited parking and drivers are advised to stop here: the jeep road continues all the way to the hut.

At the Lancet bridge, 2040m, cross the Drance and follow at a level high above the stream on its E side. Shortly after a fork in the track (where a R branch leads down to the stream again before climbing up to the Grand Chermontane huts on the other side - our route for tomorrow over the Col de Fenêtre) take a steep, unmarked path E and SE, zig-zagging up the side of a knoll and making a short cut of the jeep road. The path passes through pastures and past two small tarns and within sight of shepherd's huts, then soon reaches the Chanrion Hut, 2462m.

Option 2

Cross the Barrage (no entry for vehicles) and take a jeep track above the E bank, passing at first through tunnels (illumination unnecessary). This track ends after one hour at 2313m. A good path continues to the Lacs de Tsofeiret, set among pastures, and the Col de Tsofeiret (map marked 2642m, but signposted 2635m). (2hr 15min. from Mauvoisin. 1hr 50min. for return). There are good views of the Grand Combin from here.

A steep descent for 40m down a gully, partly protected by a chain handrail, is followed by a traverse over scree and stone blocks forming the terminal moraine of the Brenay Glacier. When a jeep track is reached on the far side of the moraine the path continues S amongst knolls and rocky outcrops to reach the Chanrion Hut in 30min. (40min. for return to Col de Tsofeiret).

The Chanrion Hut stands on an island of greenery, dotted with rocky outcrops and small tarns, and surrounded by mountain summits, glaciers and moraines. The hut commands magnificent, though limited, views to the S and W.

To the S is the obvious Col de Crête Sèche, 2899m, above the glacier of the same name. To the L of it is the Bec du Chardoney, 3447m, and to the R of it is Mont Gélé, 3518m. The Fenêtre de Durand, 2797m, is hidden from view, and to the R of the depression is Mont Avril, 3347m, almost SW of the hut. The Glacier du Mont Durand sweeps down towards the hut from the WSW, while to the W is the immense mass of the Grand Combin, 4314m.

A century and a half ago the glaciers of Brenay and Durand joined each other in the bottom of this valley and the traveller had to cross them to reach Chanrion. Forbes commented on this when he came this way in 1842. He and his party had spent the night in some humble chalets at Toremmbey, now submerged by the lake. They had a bad night: *"...we had hoped that here we should have escaped the*

The Grand Combin

The Grand Combin is third only in height to Mont Blanc and Monte Rosa and itself has several distinct summits over 4000m. One of these - the Aiguille de Croissant, 4243m - was climbed by four parties in 1857-58 but the true summit was not reached until 30 July 1859. The normal approach is from the Panossière Hut, 2669m, above the Corbassière Glacier, the longest glacier in the Western Pennines: the hut was destroyed by avalanche in spring 1988, but reopened in 1991.

---

torments of a bad bed - I mean the vermin." They were astir by 5am but it was half past six before they had breakfasted, made up their baggages, and left. Soon the valley opened *"into a scene of greater majesty than it had yet presented. A corner was turned, the valley trending more to the south-east, and several glaciers hitherto concealed came into view."*

Forbes noted that four glaciers descended the Chermontane valley. The first visible on the right hand, the Glacier de la Tsessette *"descended in 1821, as our guide (Jean Pierre) Felley informed us, so far into the valley as to approach the torrent. It has now retreated to a great height on the mountain side."* On the opposite, or eastern bank, the vast Brenay Glacier had left behind an enormous frontal moraine but *"we were assured that, in 1822, (the glacier) had extended so far as to cross the torrent, which made its way under it and to raise to a great height on the western side."* A little farther on *"it was impossible to avoid"* the Glacier du Mont Durand, descending from the Grand Combin. *"This glacier crossed, we arrived at the upper chalets of Chermontane* (Grand Chermontane, 2253m) *at the foot of the glacier of the same name* (now known as the Otemma Glacier) *which fills the entire head of the Val de Bagnes, and nearly*

48

touches the Mont Durand Glacier.

"The year 1818 had been remarkable for the extension which most of the glaciers in Switzerland had experienced after a series of cold winters." By the time of Forbes' visit in 1842 the glaciers had already retreated, and when Tuckett and Buxton came this way in 1861 they had retreated even further.

Ascents of Nearby Peaks

From the Chanrion Hut there are ascents of three nearby peaks offering superb views of the country about to be entered:

1. **Pointe d'Otemma, 3403m**

   The nearest to the hut, which may be easily ascended in 3hr by nothing more than scrambling by way of its rocky W face and S arête.

2. **La Ruinette, 3875m**

   This is a more serious climb and not for the non-mountaineer. The peak can be reached in 4hr via the Col de Tsofeiret and Col de Lire Rose and then by climbing up to and following the S arête of the peak, a short cut being taken across the uppermost snows to the foot of the rocky SW ridge, by which the summit is attained. It is possible for mountaineers to follow the NE arête to the Mont Blanc de Cheilon, 3869m, in another 4hr.

3. **Mont Avril, 3346m**

   Easily gained from the Fenêtre de Durand. (See next Section).

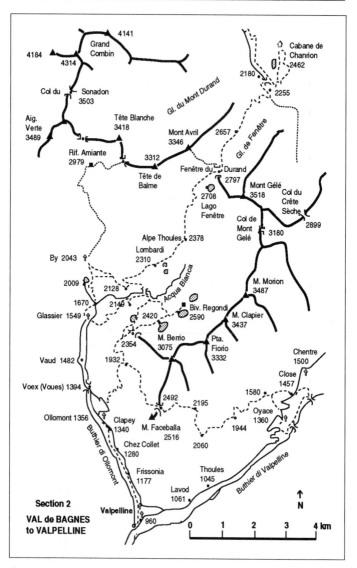

Section 2

**VAL de BAGNES
to VALPELLINE**

SECTION 2
VAL de BAGNES to VALPELLINE

The great Glacier d'Otemma (or Haut-emma) at the head of the Val de Bagnes is by far the finest of those flowing into the valley. It is about 12.5km (7.75mls) in length by 1km (1.5mls) in breadth. The Chanrion Hut stands at the western end of a steep range which bounds it on the NW, crowned by the Pointe d'Otemma, 3403m, and the Pigne d'Arolla, 3796m. On the SE it is guarded by an equally steep and lofty, but far less known range, the chief summits of which are the Mont Gelé, 3518m, the Bec de Chardoney, 3447m, the Bec d'Epicoune, 3528m, the Aiguille Tseuque, 3554m, the Grand Blanchen, 3678m, and La Singla, 3714m, forming the frontier of Switzerland with Italy.

The glacier, and the frontier ridge, provided one of the last and greatest obstacles to exploration of the Western Pennines. On the faith of statements made by the hunters of the Val de Bagnes the early travellers who visited this region were led to believe that the head of the Otemma Glacier was barred by an impassable ridge of rocks, called the Crête a Collon, forbidding all passage from the Bagnes valley eastwards from its head. In the early 1860s the Swiss mountaineers devoted their attention to the peaks on the N and S of the Otemma Glacier while English climbers chiefly devoted their attention to the discovery of a continuous 'High Level Route' from Chamonix to Zermatt.

The traverse of the Col 'Oren, 3262m (N of La Singla), by Tuckett and his party (F.F.Tuckett, J.J.Bennen, P.Perren, and C.H. & W.F.Fox) on 26 June 1861 and that of the Col de Chermontane, 3053m, a few days later by Sir T.F.Buxton's party (Sir T.F.Buxton, Mr. J.J.Cowell and Mr. E.N.Buxton with Michel Payot of Chamonix on 16 August 1861) finally disproved the existence of any such barrier, and thus opened to alpine travellers one of the grandest highways through the Pennine Alps. The supposed barrier probably owed its fabulous existence to the fact that, looking up from the foot of the Otemma Glacier the point now called Petit Mont Collon, 3555m, and its neighbours seemed to block the way towards the route of the well-known Col de Collon, 3087m, which had been discovered before 1842.

Other passes over the frontier chain were not discovered or used until much later, principally by mountaineers en-route to their flanking peaks: the Col E. de Blanchen, c3560m (between the Grand Blanchen and the Bec de la Sasse); the Col d'Otemma, 3209m (E of Aiguille Tseuque); the Col du Chardoney, 3185m (between the Bec de Chardoney and Tourme des Boucs, first traversed on 21 July 1866); the Col de Crête Sèche, 2899m - although this had been described by the Duke of Savoy's official P.A.Arnod in his report dated 1691-1694 - and the Col d'Ayace, 3040m (1km SW of the Col de Crête Sèche).

Most of these passes are now little used, except by mountaineers: the most frequently used is the Col de Crête Sèche, barely distinguishable as a col. It provides an easy passage from the Val de Bagnes to Bionaz in the Valpelline and is likely to be used more by climbers than 'tourists' like us.

The only true pedestrian pass across this frontier ridge is the Fenêtre de Durand, 2797m (formerly known as the Col du Fenêtre). It seems to have been known from very early days and has certainly been used since the Middle Ages as a means of crossing the mountain range from the Rhône valley to the Aosta valley.

The Fenêtre de Durand is the route we take to cross the frontier from Switzerland into Italy, leading us SW into a side valley of the Val Pelline. If we continue down this side valley, through the village of Ollomont, we come to the village of Valpelline in the main valley of the same name. This main route is described in Section 2.1. There is an alternative route from Ollomont to the middle reaches of the main valley above the village of Valpelline, and this is described in Section 2.2.

Both routes are shown on LS Sheets 283 Arolla and 293 Valpelline; on Kompass Sheet 87 Breuil/Cervinia - Zermatt and on IGC Sheet 5 Cervino/Matterhorn & Monte Rosa.

SECTION 2.1
FENÊTRE de DURAND, 2797m

Distance:	**20km to Valpelline**	
	(32km to Bionaz)	
Height Gain:	**617m to Valpelline**	
	(1263m to Bionaz)	
Height Loss:	**2119m**	
Grade:	**3****	

Outward		G.B.T.	Return	
		Chanrion Hut, 2462m	**7hr 30**	**2hr**
2hr 15	**2hr 15**	**Fenêtre de Durand, 2797m**	**5hr 30**	**1hr 40**
1hr 10	**3hr 25**	**Alpe Thules, 2378m**	**3hr 50**	**1hr**
25min.	**3hr 50**	**Balme, 2128m**	**2hr 50**	**40min.**
35min.	**4hr 25**	**By, 2009m**	**2hr 10**	**40min.**
1hr 50	**6hr 15**	**Ollomont, 1356m**	**1hr 30**	**1hr 30**
1hr 15	**7hr 30**	**Valpelline, 960m**		

From the SW corner of the terrace in front of the Chanrion Hut descend the footpath S to where it joins a section of sharp bends in the jeep track coming up from the Lac du Mauvoisin. Short-cuts avoid the track and you descend to the main valley to join it again as it runs northwards. Go N along it for a short way then descend to the concrete bridge crossing the main Drance stream at 2180m. (20 min. from the hut).

On the other side take the jeep track first NW then S in one big zig-zag to the Grand Chermontane chalets, 2255m. These are occupied only for about six weeks in July and August and are now not needed for accommodation as they were 150 years ago.

Forbes came this way on 15 August 1842:

"We gradually ascended towards the Col de Fenêtre, always on turf, and without any difficulty. The ascent was tedious, and we

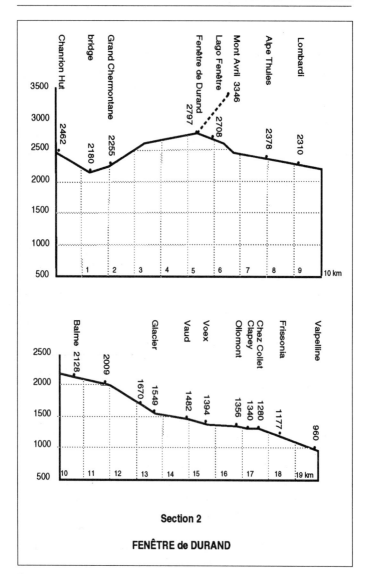

Section 2

FENÊTRE de DURAND

skirted the glacier without going upon it for the greater part of the way. The Glacier de Fenêtre is but little inclined or crevassed; in its higher part we traversed a portion of it without difficulty, so as to gain the Col more quickly. We reached the summit in four hours of easy walking from Toremmbey." (now submerged beneath the waters of Lac du Mauvoisin).

The ice has retreated considerably since then and now a well-marked path makes an easy ascent. Behind the chalets fork R and go up the grassy slopes in several zig-zags in a SW direction to a little stream at the top of the Plan Petit Giètro, c2520m, which points the way clearly upwards at a moderate gradient into the trench (at 2657m) between the Mont Avril ridge and an old lateral moraine bordering the Fenêtre Glacier. The path goes up this trench, or along the top of the grassy moraine, without possible error (cairns) to the stony slopes, passing (or through) snow patches between rocky bands and finally passes R(N) of a snow mound marking the Col, 2797m. On the ascent there are superb views looking back up the immense Otemma Glacier which Forbes had described as *"a magnificent sea of ice, nearly or quite unexplored."*

The summit of the pass is a fairly narrow ridge of bare slaty, rubbishy rock and marked by a wooden cross. Nearby are the ruins of an old hut, a control post formerly occupied by the "préposés" (border guards) set up in 1688 by order of the Duke of Savoy then seeking to prevent the Waldensians from re-entering their native valleys near Turin. An army is said to have crossed the pass in 1476 and Calvin is said to have escaped over it in 1536 from persecution in Aosta where he had been established for five years trying to reform the Aostans.

The views from the Fenêtre de Durand are extremely fine, especially on the Italian side. Beyond Aosta are the many summits in the Graians spread out in the distance, from Mount Emilius to the glaciers of the Rutor. Immediately below is the deep valley of Ollomont which is enclosed by a rugged ridge - *"a perfect ridge of pyramidal aiguilles"* (Forbes) - forming a magnificent rock wall, whose summits are named Monts Faudery, Morion and Clapier,

55

Ascent of Mont Avril, 3346m

Mont Avril lies to the NW of the Fenêtre de Durand
and can be ascended from it in 1hr 30min. over loose,
shattered, slaty rock.   It commands a fine view,
particularly of the Grand Combin and the Mont Gélé.
Mont Avril was first ascended on 20 August 1856 by
Messrs. W. & C. E. Mathews.

---

while to the W it is bounded by the craggy battlements of the entire
breadth of Mont Velan and the long line of rocky peaks extending N
and NE to the Grand Combin.

The descent from the Fenêtre de Durand on the Italian side is very
easy.   Forbes came this way in 1842 and since then other British
explorers followed in his footsteps.   The Rev. King came up the
Valpelline from Aosta in August 1855 and one day climbed up to this
pass and descended again.   On the summit of the pass he saw that
*"the tops of Mont Avril, to our right, were capped with rocks on most
fantastic fashion, one recalling exactly The Cobbler on Loch Lomond.
On the flank of Mont Gélé an enormous accumulation of disrupted
fragments lay piled up as they had fallen from the splintered crags
above. On this rested a miniature glacier, the melted ice trickling into
a little basin or lake at the foot of a wall of snow about 30ft. high? The
little lake had no visible outlet, a small moraine barring it in; and its
motionless waters, in which icebergs were floating, had a singularly
lone and mournful aspect."*

Broken rocks and debris and stone or snow slopes (according to the
season) are crossed by a mule path skirting the SE slopes of Mont
Avril passing along the N side of the icy Lago Fenêtre, 2708m.

*"In the mid-day sun the tints of the surrounding scene were all
changed, and toned down to a softer character.   The hard, stern
shades of the early morning had vanished.   Mont Gelé and its
attendant peaks were of a pale lilac grey, beautifully shaded with blue
- the strange little lake,* (the Lago Fenêtre) *at the foot of the snow*

Ascent of Mont Gelé, 3518m

The NW face of Mont Gelé rises grandly opposite Mont Avril. The frontier ridge from the pass to the summit is a difficult climb. This face was first climbed in 1899, though the summit was first reached from the S side on 11 August 1861 by F. W. Jacomb.

On 10 August 1861 Jacomb and his party walked up from Aosta to Oyace. The next day, leaving at 2am, they walked towards Bionaz and climbed into the Combe de Crête Sèche, reaching the Col de Crête Sèche at 7am.

"We remained on the Col an hour, examining those points of the 'High Level' route (i.e. the Glacier d'Otemma and its bounding ranges), and discussing the best way of attacking the Mont Gelé." After a difficult traverse, involving descents and detours, they reached the summit in 3hr. They sheltered amongst some rocks below the snow dome *"and remained there two hours, in enjoyment of the superb view around us."* They recorded the temperature and *"we built up a wall of stones between two of the huge slabs of rock and covered the aperture with a flat stone, previously depositing therein ... a thermometer, marked 'Alpine Club No. 384' together with accompanying bottle and register paper, for registry of the thermometer by any future traveller. The requisite notice of its position was posted up at Aosta and other convenient places."*

They left at 1pm and at 2.30 *"we reached the lower part of the Col du Fenêtre"* (The Fenêtre de Durand).

"We passed the little lake and the Chalets de la Balme, joined our former route from the Col du Sonadon" (which they had used a few days earlier), passed through Ollomont and Valpelline where *"the*

> *natives expressed themselves much delighted at our*
> *success and safe return."* Taking the lower road they
> entered Aosta at 7.10pm where they found *"Mr.*
> *Mathews sufficiently recovered to attack the Graian*
> *Alps, which we accordingly did the following*
> *morning."*

slope (had changed from blue-green of the morning to) *a brilliant*
opaque green." (King).

The mule path continues in a SW direction through grass and stony
slopes for a descent of 200m then turns S on a delightful course
through a boulder-field. At the first main stream (useful 'howff' under
a large boulder) the path follows a tributary and zig-zags down (path
sometimes vague) to easier ground, where tributaries from above
converge to form the Acqua Bianca stream in an alpine meadow of
emerald-green grass. Bright blue-eyed alpine forget-me-nots *Myosotis*
alpestris, Purple saxifrage *Saxifraga oppositifolia* and lovely blue
gentians dot the meadow in summer.

Follow the stream down, crossing over when you can, and in
10min. turn a corner and reach the Alpe Thoules chalets, 2378m.
(Useful shelter/bothy in bad weather).

Alpe Thoules is at the end of a dirt road. 1km beyond, just off the
road, are two tarns providing a wonderful foreground to Mont Gelé.
[By wandering SW of the two tarns you can make a short-cut to a
bridge over the Acqua Bianca stream to reach a path descending
direct to Glassier]. The track is followed past the Lombardi chalets,
2310m, and at a junction turn L downhill to the Balme chalets,
2128m.

[Just above Balme a turning L on the dirt road goes E then SE to
the Acqua Bianca stream. On the far side a path traverses above the
L bank to chalets at 2419m then descends steeply through woods and
rocks down a re-entrant valley to emerge on the E side of the hamlet
of Glassier, 1549m, at the road head].

From Balme continue on a jeep track towards By, but after 200 metres drop over the edge of the track on a path which makes a gradual descent towards a small lake (at 2009m) at the southern end of the By valley. Here, on the edge of the upper Balme and By pastures, is a splendid view commanding the whole of the Ollomont valley. You are at the head of a cul-de-sac, *"hemmed in with beetling crags of great grandeur, encircling a basin of verdant pastures, studded here and there with a few chalets."* (Rev. King).

The mountain ranges of almost the entire district of the Val d'Ollomont are composed of a metamorphic gneiss abounding in quartz. On the descent from the Fenêtre de Durand large masses of copper-stained rocks can be observed scattered about the fellsides and the valley was, until the middle of the last century, the centre of copper mining. The lake below By was dammed to provide a head of water for a crushing mill at Glassier, the remains of which can still be seen, and there are remains of other workings all the way down the valley to Valpelline.

A steep waymarked path (yellow disc, No.5, provided by the Commune of Ollomont) zig-zags down through the trees to the junction of streams with the Acqua Bianca at 1670m then turns past an old crushing mill and through pastures as a cobbled track sunken between walls to the hamlet of Glassier, 1549m, at the roadhead of the Ollomont valley.

Glassier (recently called Glacier) has a few ruined and overgrown chalets and a shrine. The former restaurant/bar is now closed. The bus stop sign is a relic of the days when bus services came this far up the valley.

It is some 3km down the road - no footpath - through the hamlets of Vaud, 1482m, and Voex, 1394m, (where there is accommodation at the Hotel Gelé at Voueces-Dessus) to Ollomont. At Voex Forbes *"found the copper works abandoned; they appear to have been very extensive and complete:"* and thirteen years later the Rev. King saw, between Voex and Ollomont *"the indication of the (copper) mines on each side of the valley, marked by heaps of bright and various coloured rubbish brought out of their bowels. ... We met numbers of*

59

sledges or trucks full of ore, drawn by men and boys harnessed with ropes. Though the descent is rapid it seemed hard work on the rude rocky track, but nearly all the ore is thus brought down to the furnaces of Valpelline."

Ollomont, 1356m, is an important village in the Valle di Ollomont, a branch of the Valpelline. There are the remains of a Roman aqueduct in the vicinity and in the last century it was the centre of copper smelting from locally mined ore. In the village centre is the parish church, dating from 1775, the bus terminus, bars and shops for supplies - fresh cheese, ham, bread, fruit, etc. - and a water trough.

Ollomont lies on the Alta Via della Valle d'Aosta No. 1 (waymarked with a red-coloured triangle and black No.1), a long-distance footpath running for 120km from Courmayeur in the W to Gressoney-St.-Jean in the E. (The AVVA No.2 runs from Courmayeur to the Gran Paradiso. Ollomont is also at the end of the five-stage AVVA No.3, running from the Valpelline to Breuil (Cervinia) at the head of the Valtournanche. We meet and follow part of it on one of the options in the next stage of this Tour). We meet and follow the AVVA No.1 in various options in the next three stages of this Tour.

In fact, the AVVA No.1 may be used as an option to get from Ollomont into the upper reaches of the Val Pelline: it all depends upon which pass you intend to take on the following day - it is another full day's walk from Ollomont to Bionaz and Prarayer. The AVVA No.1 option from Ollomont to Bionaz is described in Section 2.1.

If you don't intend to stay at Ollomont then you have to continue down the valley to Valpelline. You may wish to stay there or continue up the Val Pelline to Bionaz, or you can return to here by bus the following morning if you untend to use the AVVA No.1 option.

Buses from Ollomont to Valpelline depart from the village centre at 07.05, 12.35, 17.25, 18.25 and 20.15. Journey time is 10min. Unfortunately none of these buses continues, or connects with other buses, up the Val Pelline to Bionaz. If it is inconvenient to wait for a bus then you'll have to walk 6km into Valpelline.

From Ollomont, just beyond the village centre, take a metalled lane on the RHS through Clapey, 1340m, and as it meets another road it continues as a cart track below Chez Collet, 1280m, to Frissonia di Sopra, 1177m. Here, at the ruins of an old copper mill, the track becomes metalled again. Cross over and immediately after railings, by an electricity pole, bear R on a cart track again (junction is easily missed). This leads down, fairly steeply, to the chapel of Notre Dame of the Snows, turns an acute angle, and enters the village of Valpelline, 960m.

On the descent notice how the vegetation changes from the spruce, larch and alpine alder of the upper valley to the walnut and vines around the village.

Valpelline is the major village in the valley from which it takes its name. The village was swept away by floods of the Buthier torrent in the 16thC and subsequently reconstructed in a more secure position on its present site. In the 19thC it became an ore smelting centre and was a dirty, smoky industrial village. The Rev. King came up the valley from Aosta in August 1855 and *"at the entrance to the village I was surprised to find smoking furnaces and extensive buildings ... and other indications of large smelting works ... I found that they had been moved down to this place* (from Ollomont) *nearly two years ago, and the ore is now smelted here, in consequence of much greater facilities for obtaining wood for fuel.*

"We saw through the works, and the different stages in the process of reducing and roasting the ore, to its final issue from the furnace in bright ruddy masses of pure copper. The ore varies in richness, ranging from 20% up to as high as 85%. ... Some of the specimens of copper pyrites with quartz were very fine and pure. (The Director of the Mines) *presented us with a series of crystals of iron pyrites, from the three-faced octahedron to cubes of unusual size."*

Valpelline has all the main services, though a limited choice of shops and accommodation. There is a bar beside the bus stop in the village 'square' but most shops are on the Aosta road. The most interesting part of the village is to the N of the square, dominated by the 18thC parish church of Saint Pantaleone.

[The only other accommodation in the Val Pelline is 10km up the valley at Dzovennoz, 1575m, near Bionaz. (Two hotels and a campsite). There is now no longer any accommodation at either Oyace, 1360m, 7km further up the valley, or at Place Moulin, 1960m, 19km above Valpelline, but there is refuge accommodation beyond the reservoir at Prarayer, 2005m, 23km beyond the village.]

Having walked 20km from the Chanrion Hut it's too far today to walk up to Dzovennoz. A taxi would be expensive (enquire at the village bar) and buses are infrequent and inconvenient at this time of day - the last bus departs Valpelline to Bionaz at 17.30 (30min. journey):

Valpelline dep:	07.00	12.30	17.30
Dzovennoz arr:	07.25	12.55	17.55
Bionaz arr:	07.30	13.00	18.00

Along the valley road there are many little oratories decorated with frescoes. Each of these has the figures of two saints, painted in bright colours and often not badly executed. The favourites are St. Michael and St. Grat; St. Barbara and St. Dion; or St. Bernard and St. Ambrose.

Some 7km beyond Valpelline is Oyace, 1390m, with its polygonal 12thC tower perched on the top of a bold rock of Syenite high above the river. The rock seems to bridge the valley, but the river runs through the ravine below. The outcrop is unusual because it contrasts with the gneiss or metamorphic rocks of the valley. The village of Oyace has a 12thC church, a bar and a shop.

Between Oyace and Dzovennoz is Close, 1457m. There is now not even a bar at the former Hotel Otemma. There is no accommodation. The AVVA No.1 crosses the valley here and a signposted route over the Colle de Vessona, 2783m, is an option for us on the next stage. (See Section 3.4).

Just 2km beyond Close is Dzovennoz, 1575m, where there is accommodation - two hotels and a campsite - and 2km beyond that the bus service reaches its terminus at Bionaz, 1606m, the second andlast proper village in the valley. The 17thC church has a remarkable campanile and is in the centre of a cluster of old stone-built houses, a typical mountain village. There are few signs of tourism and it is the commune's intention to conserve the village's attractions.

Valpelline

SECTION 2.2
COL de BREUSON, 2492m

Distance:	10km, Ollomont to Close
Height Gain:	1136m
Height Loss:	1035m
Grade:	2*

Outward		G.B.T.	Return	
		Ollomont, 1356m	5hr 15	1hr 15
1hr 30	1hr 30	A. del Barrio, 1932m	4hr 30	1hr 30
1hr 30	3hr	Col de Breuson, 2492m	3hr	45min.
35min.	3hr 35	Alpe Breuson, 2195m	2hr 15	45min.
30min.	4hr 05	Sucheaz, 1994m	1hr 30	1hr 30
1hr 10	5hr 15	Close, 1457m		

This section of the route is part of the AVVA No.1 and is a relatively short stage. It has the advantage of avoiding the descent of the side valley to Valpelline and the long road walk up the main valley to Oyace. From Oyace a 2km walk up the valley is needed before you come to any accommodation.

At Ollomont, 1356m, signs say that it is 3hr 45min. to the Col de Breuson but this can easily be achieved in 3hr of actual walking. The signs also suggest that 3hr 05min. are required for the descent to Close, 1457m, but the descent can comfortably be done in 2hr 15min.

From Chef-Lieu, the centre of Ollomont, go up the lane between the primary school and the church (not immediately signposted: it starts opposite the village shop, open 0800-1300 and 1430-1930). Cross a metalled road and note that the Col is signed as being 4hr. away! Our route is waymarked Nos. 6 and 7 as far as Alpe del Berrio.

The Col de Livournea, 2858m, with the Bivacco Franco Nebbia, 2610m, (L)
and the Bivacco Luca Reboulaz, 2590m, (R) (Section 3)

A good but narrow track climbs steeply up through the woods by seemingly endless zig-zags, with the Incliousa gorge below you on your L. It comes into a clearing, when you can look down upon Ollomont, then passes a water tank at c1800m (1hr), descends slightly then climbs up again and into the meadows of the working farm of Alpe del Berrio, 1932m. (Water).

The way forward on Path No. 7/AVVA No.1 is not immediately obvious - the waymarking is poor - but turn R and diagonally upwards to meet a terrace. Go along this then climb up through the larches, eventually coming to another terrace, where there are signs of a former building c2200m (1hr after the farm). Turn L at the end of the terrace and go uphill: the path is narrow and zig-zags steeply.

The Col de Breuson, 2492m, is on a very narrow cocks-comb ridge. There is no shelter. The view is magnificent, covering all the ground on the east side of the Val Pelline from the Dent d'Hérens, 4171m, in the NE to Mont Faroma, 3073m, in the SE.

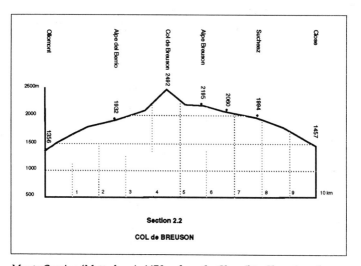

Section 2.2

COL de BREUSON

Monte Cervino (Matterhorn), 4478m, from the Cheneil to Chamois path, Valtournanche (Section 4)

The first 75m of descent (now Path No. 2 in the Comune of Oyace) are as steep as the last part of the ascent, but then the gradient eases and the path traverses round the Breuson coomb. Alpe Breuson, 2195m, is seen ahead and is soon reached. (Becoming ruinous. Basic shelter. Water nearby).

Continue the traverse beyond the old farm into the larch woods (do not be tempted to climb up to the ruins of Plan Mule, 2237m). The path becomes better and swings round the hillside and descends to the suins of Sucheaz, 1994m, on a little sunny platform with a superb view up the valley to the barrage of Lago di Place Moulin and across to Becca Morion, 2719m, directly opposite. (Sucheaz is becoming ruinous. Basic shelter. No water).

Continue the descent through the trees. The path is not marked on some maps, but it is waymarked. At the crossing of the first stream gully (washouts likely) there is a bird's eye view down to Oyace and its medieval tower. When you reach the second major gully descend so far then cross over L to just below a ruined building on the far side. (You might cast doubts on the accuracy of the waymarks as a direct descent seems obvious). The path still trends E and is heading for the mansard-roofed, whitewashed, five-storey building at Close, formerly an hotel. The path is indistinct across old meadows, crosses a dirt track, continues on the same line as before and meets a second dirt track. Turn L here then soon turn R, on a path between old stone walls leading directly into the centre of Close, 1457m. (Water).

The tall building on the L was formerly the Hotel Otemma. The bar closed a long time ago. The bus stops here: a service goes up to Bionaz at 17.55 and down to Valpelline at 18.10, but it is only a half hour walk for the 2km up to Dzovenno for accommodation.

SECTION 3
VALPELLINE to VALTOURNANCHE

The Val Pelline is a deep-cut trench, one of the longest in the Pennine Alps, and the only considerable one which does not run nearly due N and S. It runs parallel to the Italian Val Veni - Val Ferret valleys below Mont Blanc and is almost the same length - 29km/18mls. It is occupied by the main branch of the Buthier which flows from NE to SW and unites at the village of Valpelline with the other Buthier stream from the Val d'Ollomont. The combined rivers are joined by the torrent of the Artanava descending from the Gran St. Bernard, which then flow S to Aosta.

The valley has easy and direct access from Aosta but it has never been so busy or commercialised as the valleys of the Valtournanche, Gressoney or Sesia to the E. Although the upper reaches of the valley held some of the keys to the High Level Route - the Col Collon and the Col de Valpelline - and was visited by Forbes in 1842 it is relatively remote from other valleys and its attractions have been concealed. Nevertheless, there are many passes leading from the Val Pelline: those over the frontier watershed into Switzerland are across glaciers and snowfields and are the domain of the mountaineer, while those to the E, to the Valtournanche, are generally long and arduous.

The range of mountains which separates the Val Pelline from the Valtournanche is perhaps the most extensive of the lateral ridges branching off the main watershed of the Pennine Alps. It starts at the Dent d'Hérens, 4171m, and runs S with a number of high summits - Les Jumeaux, 3872m, Chateau des Dames, 3488m, and Mont Redessau, 3253m. At Mont Redessau the main ridge splits into two, enclosing the St. Barthélemy valley and preventing it from reaching the main watershed of the Alps.

The ridge to the W is by far the most important because not only does it still enclose the Val Pelline but it has the highest summits: the Becca de Luseney, 3504m, is the highest.

67

This W ridge is furrowed on the E by two side valleys - the Combe Deche and the Combe Chaleby - through which lead the easiest passes from the Val Pelline - the Col de St. Barthélemy and the Colle de Vessona, both from Oyace, while four other passes across the N half of this ridge take the walker, or mountaineer, from Bionaz or Prarayer to Valtournanche.

All of these passes (apart from the Col de Valcournera) will involve you entering the St. Barthélemy valley, a very picturesque valley and comparatively little known. You have then got to get out of that valley by crossing the ridge that runs southwards from Mont Redessau in order to get to the Valtournanche. Though seven passes cross the W ridge to get into the St. Barthélemy there are only two passes out of it to the E - the Fenêtre di Tzan, 2734m, and the Col Fenêtre, 2182m, both easier than any of those over the W ridge. By these two passes the Torgnon basin is reached, then the middle reaches of the Valtournanche are gained by crossing a spur of Mont Ersa.

Any crossing of the main ridge from the village of Valpelline to Paquier, the main village of the Valtournanche, is at least 13hr, requiring a very early start in order to reach Valtournanche at a reasonable hour. Alternatively the journey has to be split into two days: if going over the Col de Valcournera you will need a day to walk up the Val Pelline to the rifugio at Prarayer, then another day for the crossing of the pass. Using the other routes will require overnight accommodation in hotels in Lignan, the main village in the Barthélemy valley, or bivouac huts in the upper reaches of the Barthélemy valley. The crossing of the main ridge is hard and steep and the approaches to the crossings are made awkward through shortage of accommodation and transport in the Val Pelline valley. The further N the ridge is crossed the shorter the crossing, but the passes are higher and steeper: conversely, farther S the passes are lower and the distance is longer.

If weather and/or snow conditions are bad it is best to take the southernmost crossings, but if they are really bad it would be wisest to take a bus down to Aosta, then another to Châtillon, then a third up the Valtournanche.

As can be surmised from the above, there are several possible crossings of the main ridge between the two valleys, most of which involve the crossing of a subsidiary valley. There are some seven passes across the main ridge but two of them, two of the three highest passes, are mountaineers' passes and outside the scope of this guide: the Colle de Luseney, 3162m, and the Col de Cuney, 2952m. A third pass, though the easiest - the Colle de St. Barthélemy, 2645m - is too far S to be of any practical use. From N to S, therefore, the most practical passes for walkers/scramblers are:

Section	Pass	Height	Grade	Quality
3.1	Col de Valcournera	3066m	5	***
3.2	Col de Livournea	2858m	4	**
3.3	Col Montagnaya	2899m	3	**
3.4	Colle de Vessona	2783m	2	*
3.5	Fenêtre di Tzan	2734m	2	
3.6	Col Fenêtre	2182m	1	

All routes in this Section are on LS Map 1:50,000 Sheet 293 Valpelline, IGC Sheet 5, Cervino/Matterhorn & Monte Rosa and Kompass Sheet 87 Breuil/Cervinia - Zermatt.

Section 3.1 describes the whole route from the Valpelline to the Valtournanche, from Bionaz to Paquier.

Sections 3.2 and 3.3 describe the routes from the Valpelline to the Fenêtre di Tzan at the head of the Val de St. Barthélemy. For the continuation of these routes see Section 3.5.

Section 3.4 describes the route from the Valpelline to the village of Lignan in the Val de St. Barthélemy. For the continuation of this route you have the option of using the routes described in Sections 3.5 or 3.6.

From the head of the Val de St. Barthélemy it takes about 6hr to get into the Valtournanche, and unless bivouac accommodation is taken in the vicinity there is at least another 3hr of walking to be done down the Val de St. Barthélemy to get accommodation at Lignan or 4hr to Mongnod/Torgnon after crossing the Col Fenêtre.

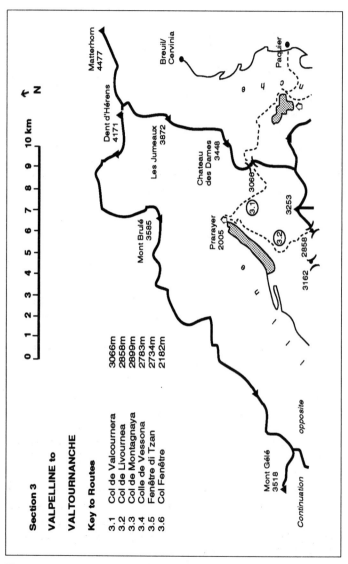

Section 3

VALPELLINE to

VALTOURNANCHE

Key to Routes

3.1	Col de Valcournera	3066m
3.2	Col de Livournea	2858m
3.3	Col de Montagnaya	2899m
3.4	Colle de Vessona	2783m
3.5	Fenêtre di Tzan	2734m
3.6	Col Fenêtre	2182m

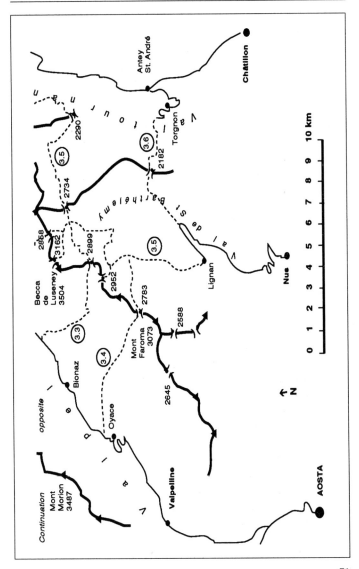

The Key to the High Level Route

The head of the Valpelline is closed in by the extensive Haut Glacier de Tsa de Tsan occupying an upland valley shut in by the Dents des Bouquetins, 3670m, on the W, by the Tête Blanche, 3724m, on the N and by the Tête de Valpelline, 3802m, and the ridge running S of the Dent d'Hérens, 3918m, on the E.

Important passes through this seemingly impenetrable headwall were first made in 1861 and 1862 to connect the Valpelline with Arolla and Zermatt. For twenty years before the discovery of the Col de Valpelline travellers passing from Aosta had two routes open to them:

1. a) via the Val Tournanche and over the St. Théodule Pass;
    b) or from the Valpelline to the Valtournanche over the intervening ridge, and then over the St. Théodule Pass
        - in either case, a long way round.
2. From the Valpelline via the wild and dreary Comba d'Oren to the Col Collon, and then down to Arolla, a route which was first traversed by Forbes in 1842, and to Evolène, and then, in a second day's hard work, over the Col d'Hérens to Zermatt.

This latter route was frequently to be preferred, as it afforded two fine glacier expeditions. But it involved a long detour - along two sides of a triangle, instead of the direct line at its base.

In the course of a series of expeditions, principally around Zermatt, in 1860 Jacomb *"had been struck with the manifest indirectness of these routes. It seemed to me that, if a passage could be made direct to Prarayer* (at the head of the Valpelline) *along the base of the triangle, and in one day instead of two, not only would the facility of access to the Chamonix district be sensibly improved, but the first link in the chain of an entirely new route be satisfactorily forged."*

Jacomb had observed the Col de Valpelline from the Col d'Hérens, but as the former is some 100m higher he had no idea of what obstacles might exist on the further side. *"It was impossible to foresee: for, being untrodden, nothing was known of them"* (i.e. the snow fields of the Haut Glacier de Tsa de Tsan).

Jacomb, with Johann Kronig and Peter Taugwald, both of Zermatt, and Franz Andermatten of Saas, therefore crossed over the St. Théodule Pass to Breuil and on the following day over the chain from the Valtournanche to the Valpelline. (See Section 3.1). The following day, on 12 August 1860, Jacomb's party set off from Prarayer at 5am up the valley and on up the glacier. As they approached the ice cliffs they were forced on to the rocks to the E - probably the same route as taken today up to the Rifugio Aosta and the Col de la Division.

But bad weather and nil visibility in mist forced them back down to Prarayer. They were off again the following morning, leaving at 5.45am *"and gained the gap in the rocks at 9.45, being little more than half the time consumed the previous day."* In another hour they were at the Col de Valpelline although *"the toil was great, owing to the increased depth of snow, and the almost insupportable heat and glare. At our left hand, or north, rose the beautiful snow top of the Tête Blanche ... we should have plenty of time left to reach Zermatt (the Col d'Hérens lies just E of it, and the route down to Zermatt is old ground), and so complete the pass, even allowing for unforeseen difficulties, and yet ascend the Tête Blanche ... and what mountaineer, finding himself so near a peak which he* has time to ascend, can resist doing so. There was the additional attraction of its being a new mountain - that is, not previously ascended." From the Col they went straight up the Tête Blanche - a climb of about 150m - and back, in an hour.

Sir T.F. Buxton and Tuckett crossed the Col de Valpelline the following year.

Jacomb's discovery of the Col de Valpelline was a significant key to the unlocking of the secrets of a High Level Route. *"I felt that this new pass ... might be appropriately named Col de la Valpelline, which name it thereupon received. It has been crossed several times since"* he wrote later *"and when more generally known, it will probably become a favourite, not only for the superb snow and glacier scenery which it offers, but at being, firstly, a not unworthy rival to the Col de Collon, in passing from Aosta to Evolène; secondly, a communication between (the Chermontane chalets and Zermatt) as conjectured by Messrs. Buxton and Cowell; and thirdly, the most direct route between the two principal points of interest, the centres of the chains of Monte Rosa and Mont Blanc, and a link of the 'High Level' route, the first in order of time, though the last in the present sequence, which the expedition of this day thus forced.*

"And so, at 5.30 pm, we strolled into Zermatt ... We had in less than 12 hours, not only affected a pass between points which had hitherto occupied two long and hard days, but had also ascended a mountain en route, and loitered away two hours of the time. It will be seen therefore, that the Col de Valpelline may be comfortably traversed in about 10 hours, with an hour additional if the ascent of the Tête Blanche is included in the excursion."

Two weeks after Jacomb crossed the Col de

Valpelline the Col du Sonadon (on the SE flank of the Grand Combin) was discovered, thereby enabling the party of Messrs. Hardy, Prest, Johnson and Hudson to make the first High Level Crossing.

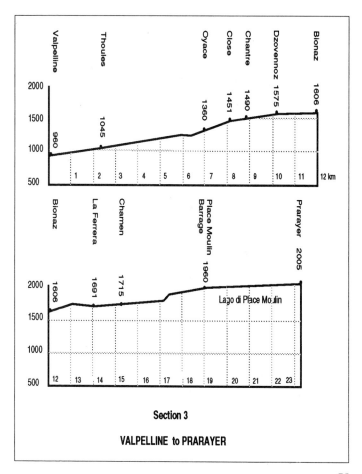

Section 3

VALPELLINE to PRARAYER

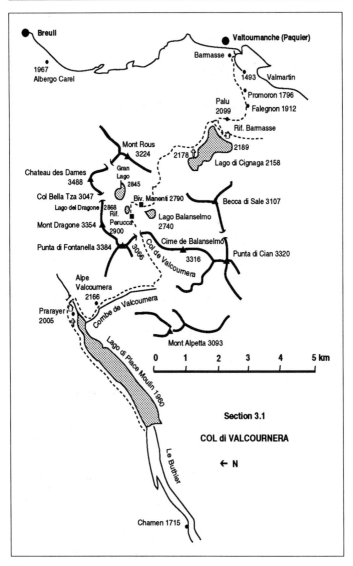

Section 3.1

COL di VALCOURNERA

← N

Distance:	**14km from Prarayer**
	(25km from Bionaz)
Height Gain:	**1129m (1528m from Bionaz)**
Height Loss:	**1603m**
Grade:	**5*****

Outward		G.B.T.	Return	
		Bionaz, 1606m	9hr 45	1hr 15
1hr 30	1hr 30	**Place Moulin Barrage, 1960m**	8hr 30	1hr
1hr	2hr 30	**Prarayer, 2005m**	7hr 30	2hr
3hr 45	6hr 15	**Col de Valcournera, 3066m**	5hr 30	1hr
30min.	6hr 45	**Rif. Perucca-Vuillermoz, 2900m**	4hr30	2hr
1hr 30	8hr 15	**Rifugio Barmasse, 2189m**	2hr 30	2hr 30
1hr 30	9hr 45	**Paquier, 1528m**		

The Col de Valcournera is the northernmost pass that can be tackled by 'tourists' such as ourselves as crossings further N are across snowfields and permanent glaciers with crevasses and require mountaineering experience in the ascent/descent of rock. This pass is without difficulty for the ordinary mountaineer: it is short but steep, rocky and hard going, and is interesting by reason of the fine views it commands of the little known range on the national frontier on the W side of the Valpelline. The Col de Valcournera is also crossed by the AVVA No.3 on a stage of its route between Prarayer and Breuil. The route is waymarked with a triangle and figure 3 in yellow and black.

The pass was known to hunters as far back as the last quarter of the 17thC and was first mentioned by P. A. Arnod, an official of the Duke of Savoy, in a report undertaken between 1691-94 concerning the mountain passes around Aosta.

Jacomb had read the Rev. King's account in his *Italian Valleys of the Pennine Alps* which had reported the existence of a steep and

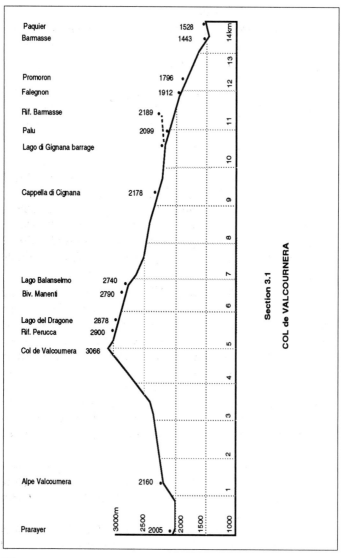

Section 3.1

COL de VALCOURNERA

difficult pass between the two valleys of the Valpelline and the Valtournanche and passing round the flank of the Chateau des Dames, and King proposed to find and cross such a pass in order to find a direct route back to Zermatt from the Valpelline.

Jacomb therefore set out from Zermatt on 10 August 1860 with Johann Kronig and Peter Taugwald, both of Zermatt, and Franz Andermatten of Saas. At Breuil (now called Cervinia, at the head of the Valtournanche) they learnt that there was indeed a pass, the Col de Valcournera, but very rarely used, and that the Chateau des Dames had never been climbed. The following day they made the first ascent of the Chateau des Dames (see below), descended and crossed the Col de Valcournera, and got down to the Valpelline at Prarayer. *"The passage of this Col ... need not occupy more than 5 to 6 hours; this is of course directly, and without diverging for the ascent of the Chateau des Dames."*

The ascent of the Col de Valcournera is best tackled from Prarayer, but it is also practical (but a very long day) from Bionaz.

Beyond the village of Bionaz, 1606m, the scenery becomes wilder. The road - there is no alternative footpath - is carried at a great height above the bottom of the deep contracted valley hanging, at one point, immediately over a precipice. After 7km (1hr - 1hr 30min.) the road ends at a large car park beside the dam wall of the Place Moulin Barrage. Stall with drinks and ices in summer. Basic toilets and tap in 'blockhouse' next to the tea hut.

A good single-track jeep road (forbidden to motorists: there's no passing/turning space until the end) continues from the N end of the dam on the W side of the lake, mostly on the level, and within an hour (on foot, 4km) you reach the chalets at Prarayer, 2005m. This is now a private rifugio (1990) with restaurant and bar.

When Forbes (in 1842), King (1850), Tuckett (1856) and Jacomb (1861) came up here the Buthier ran in a wide plain above La Lechère but it, and the hamlets of La Nuova and Les Verney, all now lie under the waters of the Lago di Place Moulin.

The emerald green pastures of Prarayer lie in a little hollow among wild mountains which close in on every side. The chalets were

79

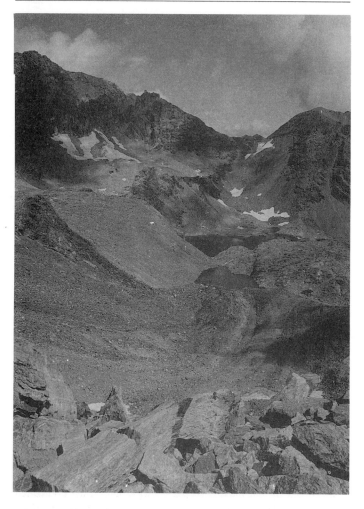

The Chateau des Dames, 3488m, and the Colle di Volfrède, 3130m, with the Gran Lago, 2845m, and the Lago del Dragone, 2868m, in the middle distance seen from the Colle di Valcournera, 3066m. The new Rifugio Piergiorgio & Corrado Vuillermoz, 2900m, is to the R of the Lago del Dragone.

constructed by the Jesuits of Aosta and stand at the far end of the verdant basin under two large rocky knolls rising in the centre of it. On the top of one is a large and conspicuous crucifix. In front, between the chalets and the lake, is the tiny chapel of La Maddelena, the last in the valley. It is now somewhat ruinous, having lost its roof. In 1649 the Jesuits became the secular canons of the Collegiate (formerly served by Austin canons regular) Church of St. Ursus at Aosta, but in 1848 this pasture was sold by them to private hands. In the summer of 1902 Mgr. Achille Ratti spent 20 days at Prarayer: in 1922 he became Pope Pious XI. As a consequence of Achille Ratti's visit a hotel was built in 1905 on a prominent knoll above the chalets, in an attempt to attract tourists. It still stands, but is shuttered and empty.

Starting from Prarayer go past the buildings and bear SE round a knoll (but not on the first track seen going R) to the Buthier torrent. A painted boulder shows Path 12 going R: follow the arrow. The bridge is much further upstream than that shown on the LK map - more E than S. A substantial plank footbridge was built in 1987 but it was damaged in spring floods in 1988 and repaired in 1989.

Traverse open, rocky ground above the torrent, entering a larch wood until you come to the Valcournera torrent. Then turn L, waymarked 12, and climb steeply uphill through woods to reach the ruined Alpe Valcournera chalets, 2166m, in 45min. (No water. There is water 10min. beyond, just after the engineered section of path, which comes from a water pipe. This is the last reliable source before the Col and before the new rifugio beside the Lago del Dragone). The Cian Glacier is in view ahead. The path lies along the stream on the R side of the Cournera glen and in another hour, at a large waymarked boulder, c2300m, it turns NE up some very steep scree. Keep to the wall on the LHS. The climb is unrelentingly steep and unpleasant. You eventually come out on to the edge of a terminal moraine, c2750m, 2hr from the valley bottom. This is the only suitable place for a rest. This is a false 'col' when seen from below, but from here the true col becomes visible, at the upper end of the couloir. Follow cairns and waymarks along the edge of the moraine, then follow a snow-filled valley. Cross the debris ahead diagonally R, to the R of the second snow patch, then make your way up to rock outcrops and finally, with relief, the pass.

The pass is no larger than 50 metres in length and is 3 metres wide. There's shelter amongst the rocky pinnacles in the middle: a small cross is on one of them. The Château des Dames, 3488m, dominates the view ahead, with Mont Rous, 3224m, to the R of the Colle di Volfrede, 3131m. The middle ground is a wild scene of glacial action. The larger and furthermost lake is Gran Lago, 2845m, with the Lago del Dragone, 2878m, the nearer, having the new Rifugio Perucca & Vuillermoz standing just above its outlet.

The descent on the other side is straight down very steep loose earth and stones for 5min. - note that the debris is about 1.0m deep, lying on ice - to the NE, towards the small Lago del Dragone, 2878m, at the head of the wild Fontanella glen, which appears to be closed to the E by the ridge stretching S from Mont Rous, 3224m. Just before you reach the lake, at 2900m, is the Rifugio Piergiorgio Perucca & Corrado Vuillermoz, erected in memory of two Cervinia guides killed on Lyskamm on 17 September 1985. It has a superb view SE to the Grand Tournalin, 3379m, across the other side of the Valtournanche. The author can certainly claim to be the first Englishman to stay here, staying overnight only three days after it was inaugurated on 4 September 1994, while builders were still working on it.

Cross the outlet to the dam of Lago del Dragone and follow the path down across glaciated rocks, reaching in 15min. the red-painted Bivacco Duccio Manenti, 2790m, a tin box erected in 1955 sleeping two people, sited beside the path just above Lago Balanselmo, 2740m. One questions whether its usefulness is now outlived and considers whether it will be removed before it becomes a refuse bin.

The path, waymarked 6, makes a zig-zag descent below the bivouac hut, crosses the stream outlet of Lago Balanselmo, passes under a cliff, recrosses the stream where it makes a fine cascade then joins the outlet of the Gran Lago at the confluence of the two streams.

(A path here goes up to Gran Lago and the Colle Bella Tza, 3047m, for the ascent of the Chateau des Dames, 3488m). The path then makes a fine traverse of a drained lake in an upper corrie, then another traverse below Mont Rous, to meet a jeep road serving the Cignana huts (water) above Lago di Cignana, 2158m. (In the summer of 1988 the lake had been drained away for repairs to be effected to the dam, but it was full again by 1990). This rough road is also signposted 'GB' meaning Grande Balconata - a five-stage/two day circuit of the Valtournanche from Cervinia. [The 'GB' , AVVA No.3 and Path No. 6B pass through the Alpe di Cignana chalets, 2260m, and cross the Finestra di Cignana, 2441m. The 'GB' makes a descent towards Avouil in the valley while the AVVA No.3 does not drop below 2000m and then climbs up to the 16-bed Bivacco Giovanni Bobba, 2770m].

Follow the farm road down to the Lago di Cignana dam - strictly, Path No. 6A takes a line below the farm road, but rejoins it nearer the dam. The Cappella di Cignana, 2178m, was built in 1966, is locked and not worth a detour. If you don't want to stay at the private Rifugio Barmasse, 2189m, across the dam, and feel you can manage the descent down into Paquier, take the path below the dam, turning R on an old railway track (used for the construction of the dam) then descend the obvious path into the valley below. (If you have visited Rifugio Barmasse you cross the outlet of the dam by a new footbridge and walk along the old railway for a short distance before descending).

The path descends past the ruined chalets of Falegnon, 1912m, and reaches the empty chalets of Promoron, 1796m, beside the half-way station of the Barmasse waterworks, 45min. from the dam.

The path, now numbered 5 & 4, leaves from the NE corner of the security fence and in another hour drops down to the valley. When you reach a t-junction, Path No. 5 goes L to the Barmasse chalets and Path No. 4 goes R - the official AVVA No.1, turning L at the next junction down to the roadhead just NE of Valmartin, 1493m. Follow the road down into the valley bottom and just beyond the bridge over the Torrente Marmore, 50m up the other side, take a path on the L which reaches the southern outskirts of Paquier village, 1528m, the main settlement of Valtournanche.

The Chateau des Dames, 3488m

An ascent of the Chateau des Dames is for mountaineers only and may be reached by way of the rocky and snowy S arête in 3hr from the Col de Volfrede, 3133m. The view from the summit is famous and very extensive. When Jacomb's party reached the top on the first ascent on 11 August 1860 they *"feasted on the splendid scene around us, increased as the enjoyment of it was by the pleasure which Alpine explorers feel on attaining the summit of a high mountain. Owing to its central position, the mountain commanded an extensive view, especially westwards, in which direction the eye enfiladed a line of snowy peaks for nearly 50 miles away, towards Mont Blanc himself. Amongst these were the Velan and Graffeneire; and nearer the Mont Gélé, Otemma, Arolla, Collon, and others, of which little was then known. ... But our principal satisfaction consisted of the fact that the position, as expected, afforded us a view over the Tsa de Tsan Glacier and concluded that a passage from the head of the Valpelline to Zermatt was possible."* (which they proved two days later).

The Chateau des Dames was described by the Rev. King as he saw it from Breuil in 1850 as *"one of the loftiest points in the ridge, and a smooth dome of snow, out of which rise some singular bare rocks; and they certainly had a remarkable resemblance to ladies marching up the snow to an Alpine castle"* whence it is supposed its name arose.

SECTION 3.2
COL de LIVOURNEA, 2858m

Distance:	**10km from Prarayer to Fenêtre di Tzan**	
Height Gain:	**1448m**	
Height Loss:	**719m**	
Grade:	**4****	

Outward		G.B.T.	Return	
		Prarayer, 2005m	6hr 30	30min.
30min.	30min.	**Montsarvin, 2194m**	6hr	1hr
1hr	1hr 30	**Lago di Livournea, 2374m**	5hr	15min.
15min.	1hr 45	**La Tsa, 2410m**	4hr 45	30 min.
45min.	2hr 30	**c2500m**	4hr 15	1hr 30
2hr	4hr 30	**Col de Livournea, 2858m**	2hr 45	1hr 30
30min.	5hr	**Lago Luseney, 2585m**	1hr 15	1hr 15
1hr 15	6hr 15	**Fenêtre di Tzan, 2734m**		

This is an inconvenient route because there is no access to the S side of the Lago de Place Moulin from the barrage and a long rising traverse from Prarayer is necessary to gain entry into the Livournea glen. The route is easy as far as the 2500m contour, but thereafter it is long and rough: there are at least two high passes to cross, so height gain and loss are considerable. However, there are three bivouac huts en route and provided you have cooking kit and food an overnight stay in one of them will enable the journey to Paquier to be done in two days.

Starting from Prarayer follow Section 3.1 as far as the Valcournera torrent, but then cross the wooden bridge on Path No. 13 and continue through the woods on the far side. The path traverses through the larch woods then climbs by a good graded path to the ruined Montsarvin hut, 2194m. (No shelter, but water). Then begins a good rising traverse on a well-graded path - used for taking cattle to the

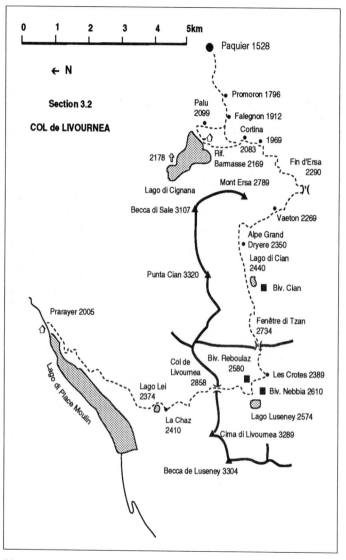

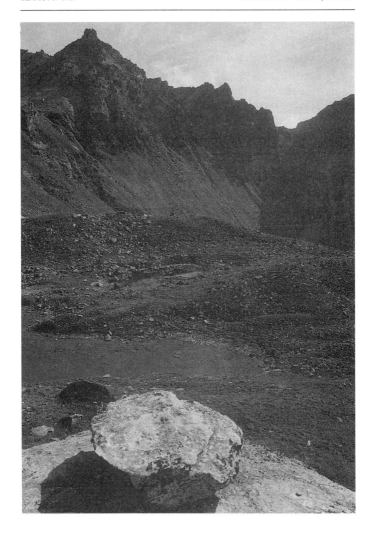

Mont Rédéssau, 3253m, and the Fenêtre di Tzan, 2734m,
seen from Lago Luseney, 2574m. The Bivacco Franco Nebbia, 2610m,
is in the centre of the picture.

Livournea glen, now that a direct route from Place Moulin is no longer possible - climbing up to 2450m before dropping down to Lago di Livournea, 2374m. Path No. 13 ends here.

Go round the inlet side of the lake (last certain chance of water) and go over the low col behind it, to pick up a path to the ruins of the La Chaz/La Tsa huts, 2410m. (Shelter in semi-underground byres. No water). Go up into the corrie basin at c2500m. The cliffs rise ahead and there appears to be no way out, but climb up the lateral moraine on the R to a point just behind its snout and follow the moraine up to the remnants of the small Livournea glacier. A route, marked by little cairns, curves in and out of glacial debris, at one point going into a narrow gully, and in parts passing small permanent snow patches. A way finally trends L along the top of a big boulder slope and leads you to the narrow gap that is the pass.

The pass is a scene of wild desolation: jagged peaks and jumbled rocks are all around. Up to the L is Mont Rédéssau, 3253m, whose W and S ridges mark the split of the main ridge into the two arms that enclose the Barthélemy valley, the R arm going down to the Fenêtre di Tzan, 2734m. Up to the R is the Cima Livournea, 3289m, and next to it the Becca de Luseney, 3304m, and the Becca d'Arbière, 3319m. Below them is a mass of red rocks forming a terminal moraine of their former glacier, while directly below them and you is the little moraine lake of Lago Luseney. Beyond and below, the trench of the Barthélemy valley begins to wind its way southwards to the Dora Baltea at Nus.

From the Col descend steeply on a route faintly marked by little cairns to the level glacial coomb below. Here is easier ground. A way is cairned, but by following any of the little streams you will come to Lago Luseney, 2574m, while the path turns L to the ruined huts of Alpe Luseney, 2585m.

Between the Luseney huts and the lake there is on the L the luxurious Bivacco Luca Reboulaz, 2580m, inaugurated on 11 September 1993 and provided with bedding and blankets for 24 people and having gas stove and cooking equiment: it is of a similar standard to the Bivacco Rosaire-Cleremont on the Colle de Vessona. The author claims to be the first English overnighter. On the top of the hillock in front of the new bivouac hut, some 400 metres away at 2610m is the Bivacco Franco Nebbia, the usual six-bed tin hut erected by the CAI in 1958. Like the Bivacco Manenti on the Col de Valcournera route one may now consider its usefulness as outlived.

The main path doesn't go to the lake but from the Luseney huts goes SE beside a stream and descends (in 15min. from the Bivacco Reboulaz) to Les Crotes, 2389m, semi-underground byres still in good condition: with stone vaulted roofs they would make good shelter. (Do not be tempted to traverse across from the bivacco to the Fenêtre di Tzan - the slope is too rocky even though there is a faint path, created by those who thought the short-cut easier. It is quicker and easier to go on the path via Les Crotes).

Les Crotes is at the head of the Val de St. Barthélemy and it is from here that this route (and the routes in Sections 3.3 and 3.4) lead to cross the Fenêtre di Tzan to get to the Valtournanche. At Les Crotes we meet the AVVA No.1 which crosses the Fenêtre di Tzan.

From Les Crotes, 2389m, there is a steep climb, up zig-zags on Path No.19 for 1hr to the Fenêtre di Tzan, 2734m. (local spelling: other spellings are Cian, Tsan and Tian). There is a steep final climb through scree to the ridge, rocky on the W side, grassy on the E, topped by a large wooden cross.

From here follow the route described in Section 3.5.

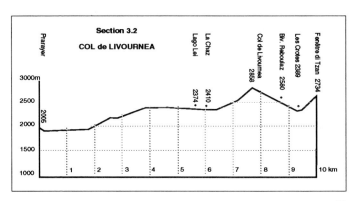

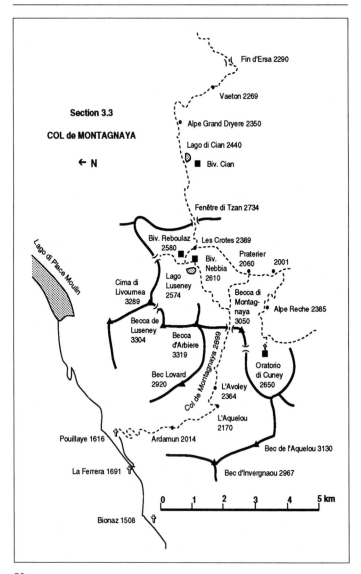

Section 3.3

COL de MONTAGNAYA

← N

Fin d'Ersa 2290

Vaeton 2269

Alpe Grand Dryere 2350

Lago di Cian 2440

Biv. Cian

Fenêtre di Tzan 2734

Biv. Reboulaz 2580

Les Crotes 2389

Biv. Nebbia 2610

Praterier 2060

2001

Lago Luseney 2574

Cima di Livournea 3289

Becca di Montagnaya 3050

Alpe Reche 2385

Becca de Luseney 3304

Becca d'Arbiere 3319

Col de Montagnaya 2899

Bec Lovard 2920

Oratorio di Cuney 2650

L'Avoley 2364

Lago di Place Moulin

L'Aquelou 2170

Pouillaye 1616

Ardamun 2014

Bec de l'Aquelou 3130

La Ferrera 1691

Bec d'Invergnaou 2967

Bionaz 1508

0   1   2   3   4   5 km

SECTION 3.3
COL de MONTAGNAYA, 2899m

Distance: **14km from Bionaz to Fenêtre di Tzan**
Height Gain: **1863m**
Height Loss: **735m**
Grade: **4****

Outward		G.B.T.	Return	
		Bionaz, 1606m	**6hr 25**	**45min.**
1hr 05	**1hr 05**	**Pouillaye, 1616m**	**5hr 40**	**45min.**
1hr	**2hr 05**	**Ardamun, 2015m**	**4hr 55**	**15min.**
30min.	**2hr 35**	**L'Aquelou, 2175m**	**4hr 40**	**45min.**
30min.	**3hr 05**	**L'Avoley, 2364m**	**3hr 55**	**45min.**
1hr 25	**4hr 30**	**Col de Montagnaya, 2899m**	**3hr 10**	**2hr**
1hr 45	**6hr 15**	**Lago Luseney, 2574m**	**1hr 10**	**1hr 10**
1hr 15	**7hr 30**	**Fenêtre di Tzan, 2734m**		
1hr 30	**6hr**	**Praterier, 2060m**	**2hr 30**	**15min.**
15min.	**6hr 15**	**La Sayvaz, 1985m**	**2hr 15**	**2hr 15**
2hr 10	**8hr 25**	**Lignan, 1633m**		

This is a reasonably good route, not as rough as Section 3.2 because the rocky bits are only in the last 500m of ascent and 200m of descent of the pass, and because of a lovely walk up the hanging valley of the Combe de Montagnaya. Nevertheless, the way to Paquier is longer and requires two days: unless you want to spend the night at the bivouac huts of Franco Nebbia or Luca Reboulaz (6hr 15min.) or Cian (beyond the Fenêtre di Tzan, 8hr 30min.) the alternative is to descend to Praterier in the Val de St. Barthélemy and go down to the village of Lignan.

Walk up the road from Bionaz, 1606m (or take the track running parallel to it from behind the village church for about 1km) for 55 min. to La Ferrera, 1691m. Leave the road and take the track winding down into the valley to the bridge over the Buthier torrent (car

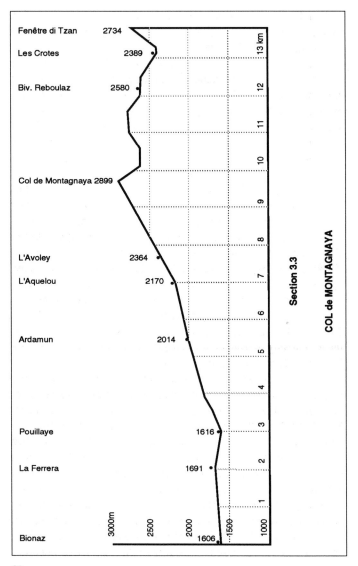

Fenêtre di Tzan 2734
Les Crotes   2389
Biv. Reboulaz   2580
Col de Montagnaya 2899
L'Avoley   2364
L'Aquelou   2170
Ardamun   2014
Pouillaye   1616
La Ferrera   1691
Bionaz   1606

13 km
12
11
10
9
8
7
6
5
4
3
2
1

3000m 2500 2000 1500 1000

Section 3.3

COL de MONTAGNAYA

park)and the whitewashed chapel and barns at Pouillaye, 1616m. Note the old spelling Poujllaye. Water supply at Pouillaye is last supply until you reach Ardamun.

Go southwards past the barns on Path No. 15 (all the way to the Col) then steeply up through woods (though pleasant, being in morning shade) and after an hour arrive at the Ardamun hut, 2014m. (Mostly ruins, but some shelter. Water). You are now out in the open and the delightful meadow immediately above the chalet, in a broad green basin, may easily tempt you to linger. A large amphitheatre of peaks enclose the basin: Becca del Merlo, 3234m, to the L, Becca del' Aquelou, 3130m, to the R, with Mont Pisonet, 3205m, to the L of centre. In 30min. more you reach the Alpe L'Aquelou hut, 2170m, (ruined, but basic shelter in stone-built barrel-shaped byre. Stream nearby is last source of water until Bivacco Luca Reboulaz is reached). In another 30min. you reach the ruined Alpe L'Avoley chalet, 2364m. (Basic shelter, but no water). Here you turn E, climbing the stony slope and soon the way to the Col de Montagnaya can be seen ahead. You can avoid any snow patches: the path is faint through grass and scree and reaches the pass in another 90min.

The pass occupies a narrow gap between the Becca d'Arbière,3319m, to the L and the Becca di Montagnaya, 3050m, to the R. Directly in front of you is the Cima Bianca, 3009m, with the Fenêtre di Tzan the obvious notch to its L.

From the pass descend a very steep stone slope. Do not be tempted into the stream gully but trend L on a faint path as close below the cliffs as possible. It crosses a spur between two gullies - the one you have just left and the one next N. Here a path goes down the steep grass spur to Praterier in the St. Barthélemy valley (see below). Turn L, N, and traverse across the coomb to the gap on the skyline ahead near Pt. 2783m. Turn N, descending to pick up a path that avoids the eastern scree slopes of Becca d'Arbière, 3319m. The Lago Luseney, 2574m, and the Bivacco Franco Nebbia, the usual 6-bed tin hut, standing on top of the moraine above its E shore at 2610m, can be seen ahead. Memorise the location of the Franco Nebbia hut and lake as there is some confusing ground to cross once you have descended to the levels of the almost-dried up streams: the hillock between you and the lake drops steeply down to the shore of the lake, making a direct approach inadvisable. Take care in fog or cloud.

The main path doesn't go to the Franco Nebbia bivouac hut but from the Luseney huts and Bivacco Luca Reboulaz goes SE beside a stream and descends, in 15min., to Les Crotes, 2389m, semi-underground byres still in good condition: with stone vaulted roofs they would make good shelter. (Do not be tempted to traverse across from Bivacco Reboulaz to the Fenêtre di Tzan - the slope is too rocky even though there is a faint path, created by those who thought a short-cut easier. It is quicker and safer to go on the path via Les Crotes).

Les Crotes is at the head of the Val de St. Barthélemy and it is from here that this route (and most of the following routes in this Section) lead to cross the Fenêtre di Tzan to get to the Valtournanche. At Les Crotes we meet AVVA No.1 which crosses the Fenêtre di Tzan.

From Les Crotes, 2389m, there is a steep climb up zig-zags on Path No.19 for 1hr to the Fenêtre di Tzan, 2734m. (local spelling: other spellings are Cian, Tsan and Tian). There is a steep final climb through scree to the ridge, rocky on the W side, grassy on the E, topped by a large wooden cross.

From here the route is described in Section 3.5.

For the exit by the St. Barthélemy valley descend the spur steeply from Les Crotes, turning L to cross a stream in a deep gully and then down more open flanks to the large farm of Praterier, 2060m.

The farm is situated in a flat area of the valley on the edge of a fine Scots pine wood and a 15min. walk on turf through trees brings you down past Ollière, 2007m, to La Sayvaz, 1985m.

La Sayvaz is on the AVVA No.1 route from the Col de Vessona and Oratorio de Cuney. A good track leads southwards past Chancombre, 1927m, and all the way to the village of Lignan, 1633m.

This exit from the route involves an additional height loss of 1266m, an extra distance of 10km and about 3hr 55min. more time.

SECTION 3.4
COLLE de VESSONA, 2783m

Distance:	17.5km from Oyace to Lignan	
Height Gain:	1722m	
Height Loss:	1466m	
Grade:	2*	

Outward		G.B.T.	Return	
		Oyace, 1457m	7hr 15	20min.
15min.	15min.	Bëtenda, 1359m	6hr 55	1hr 10
1hr 45	2hr	La Vieille, 1930m	5hr 45	35min.
50min.	2hr 50	L'Ardamun, 2206m	5hr 10	1hr 10
1hr 40	4hr 30	Colle de Vessona, 2783m	4hr	55min.
35min.	5hr 05	Plan Piscina, 2544m	3hr 05	15min.
30min.	5hr 35	Colle de Chaleby, 2683m	2hr 50	20min.
15min.	5hr 50	Col de Salvé, 2568m	2hr 30	05min.
05min.	5hr 55	Colle de Fontaney, 2568m	2hr 25	1hr 25
35min.	6hr 30	Tza Fontaney, 2079m	1hr	1hr
55min.	7hr 25	Lignan, 1633m		
40min.	6hr 30	Oratorio, 2652m	2hr	2hr
1hr 50	7hr 40	La Sayvaz, 1985m		

The Colle de Vessona is given the height of 2783m on maps, but 2789m on signposts. A number of signposts on this route have conflicting detail as to footpath numbers and intermediate times: the Comune of Oyace have recently re-painted footpath numbers on the ground and these numbers are on the latest maps. The mass of signposts on this route show that this Section (Close - Vessona - Oratorio) is part of the AVVA No.1. It is likely to be a popular route. The route starts at Close, 1457m, at the former Hotel Otemma, but the nearest accommodation now is 2km up the road at Dzovennoz.

Cross the road and go over a field on a path (signposted as No. 29, but waymarked as No. 5), across a footbridge and into the woods. At

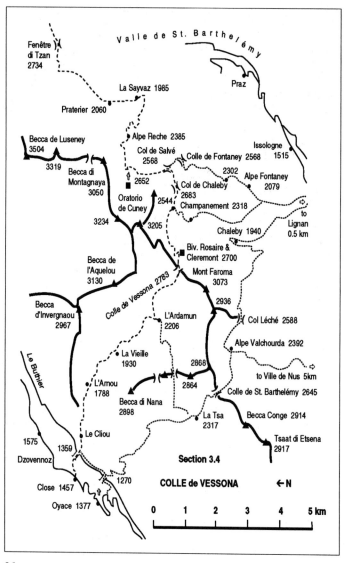

Valle de St. Barthelémy

Fenêtre di Tzan 2734

La Sayvaz 1985

Praterier 2060

Praz

Alpe Reche 2385

Becca de Luseney 3504

3319

Col de Salvé 2568

Colle de Fontaney 2568

Issologne 1515

Becca di Montagnaya 3050

2652

2302

Alpe Fontaney 2079

Oratorio de Cuney

2544

Col de Chaleby 2683

Champanement 2318

to Lignan 0.5 km

3234

3205

Chaleby 1940

Biv. Rosaire & Cleremont 2700

Becca de l'Aquelou 3130

Mont Faroma 3073

Colle de Vessona 2783

2936

Becca d'Invergnaou 2967

L'Ardamun 2206

Col Léché 2588

Alpe Valchourda 2392

Le Buthier

La Vieille 1930

2868

to Ville de Nus 5km

L'Arnou 1788

2864

Colle de St. Barthelémy 2645

Becca di Nana 2898

La Tsa 2317

Becca Conge 2914

Le Cliou

Tsaat di Etsena 2917

1575

1359

Section 3.4

Dzovennoz

1270

COLLE de VESSONA   ← N

Close 1457

Oyace 1377

0   1   2   3   4   5 km

96

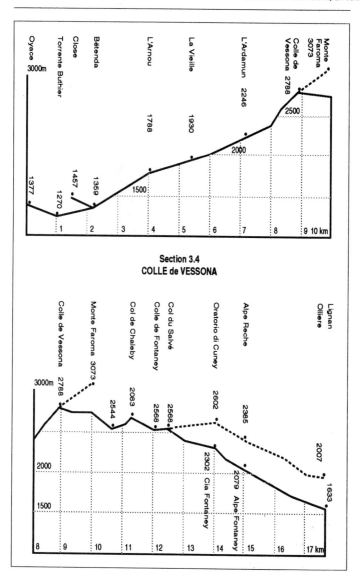

Section 3.4
COLLE de VESSONA

a T-junction turn R and descend quickly on a steep zig-zag path to a narrow stone bridge at Bëtenda, 1359m, spanning the Buthier torrent, here running in a deep, narrow chasm. The bridge was built in 1688 and now has handrails for the faint-hearted. This is a delightful spot in a glade in the woods, shady in the morning but very hot in the afternoon: if you are going in the reverse direction the climb up to the road is most tiresome in the heat of the afternoon.

[If starting from Oyace, 1377m, descend below the prominent tower on its rock to the road below and at the first hairpin bend take a track descending steeply down into the savage gorge to the Buthier torrent. Here you can go up the R bank or cross over to the L bank: the L bank is to be preferred because it is in the shade longer. Either way, follow the river upstream for 1km (if going up the L bank first go up the road on the far side for a short way, then turn off L on a path) to reach the bridge at Bëtenda, 1359m].

From the bridge at Bëtenda Path 28 makes a rising traverse up the glade to the L. After 100 metres, by a big boulder on the R (waymark arrow points downhill only and cannot be seen from below) turn R through larch woods on a good path. You come to a clearing and ruins of Le Cliou huts, c1530m (where there is the last view down to Bionaz) and into the mouth of the pretty Vessona glen. The path keeps to the L bank of the stream, passing the ruined L'Arnou huts, 1788m, seen through the larches on the far side, and through a glen where green turf and moss-covered rocks alternate with pine forest. In the glades here the noble blue Alpine columbine *Aquilegia alpina* (rare, protected) is abundant. Among the flowers are myriads of butterflies - Apollos, fritillaries, lustrous coppers and brilliant blue *Polyommati*.

The path then reaches the recently renovated farm of Le Vieille, 1930m, (water) standing in a little green plain, formerly a lake basin, unfortunately scarred by drainage works. Mont Faroma, 3073m, and the pass can now be seen clearly ahead. The pass is to the R of the pinnacles on the LH skyline. To the SE this glen is surrounded by an amphitheatre of rocks which have to be surmounted: the path goes up to the foot of the cliffs and turns away to the L of flood debris, then turns S to breach the cliffs and reach the restored L'Ardamun chalets,

2206m, (water) protected by cliffs forming the lip of a wild hollow.

The path, now Path 27, leads up over flood debris behind the hut and then climbs shifting boulder slopes to the pass.

The pass is at an altitude of 2783m, though marked 6m higher on signposts. There is no shelter on the pass, which commands a noble view, including Mont Blanc. This view may be extended by climbing the shale slopes SW for 1hr to the summit of Mont Faroma, 3073m.

Just below the Colle de Vessona on the E side, 10 min. down on Path No. 10 but just off the AVVA No.1, is the superb stone Bivacco Umberto Rosaire & Marco Cleremont standing at 2700m just above the moraine lake Lac de Champanement. Newly constructed in 1989 and inaugurated on 7 September 1989 it has 18 bunk beds and blankets, dining room and pots, pans, plates and gas stove. The author claims to be the first Englishman to have spent an overnight in this hut. The hut is clearly intended to serve long-distance walkers on the AVVA No.1, making it one of five bivouac huts on the route between the Valpelline and the Valtournanche.

Path No. 10 winds down above a line of cliffs NE then descends nearly due E over stones and through the Gruin pastures to the Plan Piscina huts, 2544m, at the head of the Chaleby glen.

[Though not the most attractive, the quickest way to Lignan, the main settlement of the St. Barthélemy valley, is by a rapid descent on Path No. 10 to the summer farm of Champanement, 2318m, then by following a jeep track carved across the Champorcher fellside making a gradual descent to the village in 1hr 30min. (2hr for ascent in reverse). The path beside the Chaleby stream, No. 105, appears to have fallen into disuse between Alpe Chaleby, 1940m, and c1779m, because of the 'new' jeep track].

From Plan Piscina, Path No.10A makes an easy climb up to the Colle di Chaleby, 2683m. There is some confusing ground between the Colle di Chaleby and the Col de Salvé, although the signpost on one can be seen from the other. Path No.10A is not evident on the ground and the route could be confusing in mist or cloud. Go S of a small tarn then over a grassy rise eastwards. The Col de Salvé, 2568m, is a broad shoulder and would not be recognised as a col were it not for its signpost.

[From the Col de Salvé the Oratorio de Cuney can be seen due N above the rocky spurs flanking the Becca Fontaney, 2971m. It is easily reached   in 40min. on Path No. 11: 6hr 30min. from the Valpelline. The Oratorio stands in a desolate, stony hollow at 2652m, wherein grows a kind of juniper, known locally as 'cuneia' which has given its name to the spot.

The Oratorio de Cuney (or Cunei, or Chiny) is a sanctuary of considerable local renown. It consists of a church, dedicated to Notre Dame de la Neige, which was founded about 1650 and was rebuilt on a larger scale in 1869. Several rooms still receive the priests who say Mass here on 5 August annually, the inhabitants of the St. Barthélemy valley coming up in a solemn procession.

Adjoining the sanctuary is a two-storied barn, the upper floor providing basic accommodation for 18 people - beds and mattresses but no blankets. The rifugio is always open but if the custodian is in residence (July to end of August) basic meals are available or he will cook your own food for you. Water trough outside.

For those who wish to continue direct from the Oratorio to the Fenêtre di Tzan it is a journey of another 4hr - although the signpost says 4hr 45min. It will take you 4hr 30min. to get to the Bivacco Franco Nebbia (9hr 10min.) or 5hr 15min. to get to the Bivacco Cian (9hr 55min.), making a long day by this route].

A shorter day and hotel accommodation is available by going S for some 2hr from the Col de Salvé on a direct and picturesque route to the village of Lignan, but be aware that vacant accommodation in the village is scarce at the best of times.

Five minutes S of the Col de Salvé, marked by a flimsy cross on a tall telegraph pole, is the Colle de Fontaney, also 2568m, with a good view back to the Oratorio and forward over the Aosta valley. The path then begins a long gradual descent across the fine Tza (or Cia) Fontaney pastures, 2302m, down to Lignan, 1633m.

There are two hotels in Lignan: the Hotel Cuney (turn R to the T-junction, then turn L) or the Hotel Luseney at Clemensod (turn R to the T-junction, then R again, then 200 metres).

100

This route from Oyace to Lignan over the Colle de Vessona was followed by the Rev. King and his party in August 1855. At the Bëtenda bridge over the Buthier he described *"... a lofty cleft in the high overhanging wall of rock, through which the torrent rushes into a dark boiling cauldron, from which all sunlight is shut out by its deep, shaft-like sides; and as we stood on the bridge the cool air, saturated with the fine spray, wafted past us with delicious freshness."*

On entering the Combe di Vessona *"... we now got a view of the sharp jagged ridge of lofty mountains, partly covered with snow, and stretching across the valley, over which was our route."*

Above the L'Ardamun chalets *"... the serrated ridge of the Col overhung us. All possible points of passage seemed the same - steep and inaccessible, except at one point, where a large bed of sloping snow promised an escape, for part of the way, from the steep slippery bed of crumbled rock, which lay at as great an angle as the stones could possibly rest.*

"Half an hour above the chalets - which we now looked down on as tiny cabins - the ascent became steep and the track narrow ... The chief difficulty of the ascent was now to come... It reminded us more of the last pull up the cone of Vesuvius than anything else, only the soft ashes and cinders of the latter are easy and comfortable climbing in comparison with the clattering mass of shaly debris which every few steps - as we plunged mid-leg deep into it - slipped bodily down with us on the steep incline, which seemed almost perpendicular... We reached the snowfield I had marked from below. On taking to it we found - though hard frozen, and excessively slippery from its great steepness - a great relief. In ordinary

seasons it is, I believe, a mere patch. Above this, the last part of the climb was a colossal pile of blocks of all sizes, one above the other, in wild confusion, over and among which we clambered, like ants on lumps of sugar. At length we reached the summit of the Col an hour and a half after leaving the chalets.

"The view which burst upon us from the narrow knife-like ridge was more than a reward for all our toil, and different from any other scene we had yet witnessed. As we climbed up there was no time to look round, and now we found the mighty form of Mont Blanc, the Grande Jorasse, and others, had risen up behind us, above a long range of peaks to the westward while the glittering heads of Mont Combin and Mont Velan, with the glaciers of Mont Gélé, and over the Crête Sèche, closed up the view to the north, giving us a perfect panorama of the well-known outlines of many familiar acquaintances, in novel and unexpected combinations.

"Turning southward to look to the other side the contrast was as remarkable as if it were a different climate and country. To the N the scene behind us was cold, stern and icy - but through the opening of the Col, framed in the high rocks on either side of us, range after range of southern Alps rose in endless waves - shutting out all view into the valleys, bare alike of snow or trees, and bathed in a soft haze of blue, purple, and olive tints.

"The descent was very striking, the beautiful southern mountain ranges blending in every varying tint of ashy purple, amethyst and rosy red, exquisitely soft and transparent for such bare ridges; and the Italian glow and warmth of colouring in the setting sun was the more enchanting in contrast with the dark, stern crags and snow peaks of the other side."

The Rev. King and his party dropped down the Chaleby valley from Plan Piscina to Lignan where they happened to arrive at a crowded inn on the eve of the festival and procession to the little chapel of Notre Dame de la Neige at Cuney.   The 'inn' no longer provides accommodation; it has a bar only. There are two, two-star hotels elsewhere in the village.

Mont Pisonet, 3205m, and Colle de Vessona, 2783m,
from L'Ardamun, 2206m

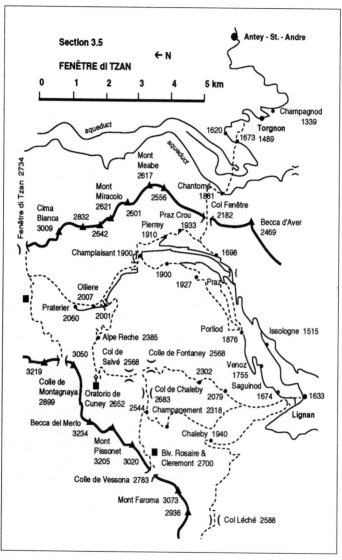

Section 3.5

FENÊTRE di TZAN

← N

0   1   2   3   4   5 km

Antey - St. - Andre

Champagnod 1339

Torgnon 1489

1620   1673

aqueduct

aqueduct

Mont Meabe 2617

Chantorne 1881

Col Fenêtre 2182

Becca d'Aver 2469

Mont Miracolo 2621

2556

2601

Praz Crou 1933

Fenêtre di Tzan 2734

Cima Bianca 3009

2832

2642

Pierrey 1910

Champlaisant 1900

1698

1900   1927   Praz

Olliere 2007

Praterier 2060   2001

Porliod 1876

Issologne 1515

Alpe Reche 2385

3050

Col de Salvé 2568   Colle de Fontaney 2568

2302

Venoz 1755

3219

Colle de Montagnaya 2899

Oratorio de Cuney 2652   2544

Col de Chaleby 2683

Champagnement 2318

2079

Saguinod 1674

1633

Lignan

Becca del Merlo 3234

Chaleby 1940

Mont Pissonet 3205   3020

Biv. Rosaire & Cleremont 2700

Colle de Vessona 2783

Mont Faroma 3073   2936

Col Léché 2588

SECTION 3.5
FENÊTRE di TZAN, 2734m

Distance:	12.5km, Fenêtre di Tzan to Paquier	
Height Gain:	454m	
Height Loss:	1588m	
Grade:	2	

Outward		G.B.T.	Return	
		Fenêtre di Tzan, 2734m	7hr 35	1hr
1hr	**1hr**	**Lago di Cian, 2440m**	6hr 35	55min.
30min.	**1hr 30**	**Grand Drayere, 2350m**	5hr 40	1hr 10
1hr 10	**2hr 40**	**Fin d'Ersa, 2290m**	4hr 30	2hr
1hr 30	**4hr 10**	**Rifugio Barmasse, 2189m**	2hr 30	2hr 30
1hr 30	**5hr 40**	**Paquier, 1528m**		

As we have seen, Routes 3.2 - 3.4 require two days for the passage from the Valpelline to the Valtournanche and, in order to get into good position for the exit from the Valtournanche, most walkers will cross the Fenêtre di Tzan. You then have to cross the Fin d'Ersa, 2290m, (the Col de Fort, 2906m, is outside the scope of this guide) to reach the outlet of the Lago di Cignana and the descent to Paquier, the principal village of the Val Tournanche.

Walkers who have found accommodation at Lignan, the main village of the Val de St. Barthélemy, will need to ascend to the head of the valley if the crossing of the Fenêtre di Tzan is the objective: a route description, map and profile are given below. However, if the Col Fenêtre is the objective, for an easy day to Mongnod/Torgnon, then you'll need to follow Section 3.6.

From the Fenêtre di Tzan, 2734m, (local spelling: other spellings are Cian, Tsan or Tian) a good mule track, numbered 18A or 71, makes an easy descent through turf between rocky valleys and ridges eastwards towards the Lago di Cian, 2440m, which it reaches in an

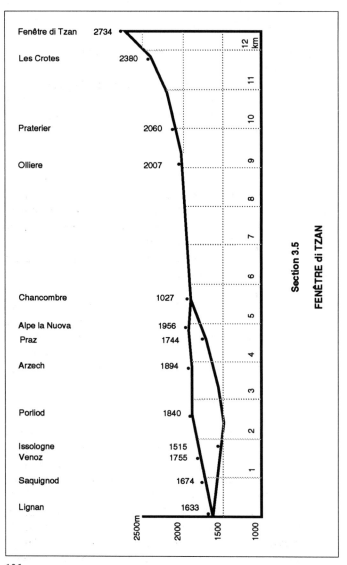

Section 3.5

FENÊTRE di TZAN

Fenêtre di Tzan	2734
Les Crotes	2380
Praterier	2060
Olliere	2007
Chancombre	1027
Alpe la Nuova	1956
Praz	1744
Arzech	1894
Porliod	1840
Issologne	1515
Venoz	1755
Saquignod	1674
Lignan	1633

hour. This large shallow tarn is a favourite bathing place for the cattle which graze the Grand Drayere pastures.

[Just to the S of the Lago di Cian is the Bivacco Cian, 2489m, reached in 10min. by a path on the W side of the lake. It is a large tin box with 9 beds, mattresses and blankets, but larger than standard and having stove, table, utensils, etc., and a water supply outside. As it is on the AVVA No.1 it is likely to be well used. It is another 3hr 20min. to Rifugio Barmasse via Fin d'Ersa].

In another 30min. from the Lago di Cian you come to the Grand Drayere huts, 2350m, at the head of the Torgnon basin. The sunny alpine pastures here lie below the headwall of the high cliffs of the Becca di Sale, 3107m, and the Punta Cian, 3320m.

From Grand Drayere continue E on the AVVA No.1 towards Mont Ersa then SE on a narrow trod to the Vaeton huts, 2269m. Then continue on a jeep road for 500 metres then turn off up L to the col of Fin (Finestra) d'Ersa, 2290m. Here you're on the treeline, among the Arolla pines, juniper and Alpine bilberry.

From the col the path, No.13, goes generally NE through the meadows and pines to an isolated farm then drops down to a jeep road. Follow this part of the Grande Balconata, but still Path 13, up to Alpe Cortina, 2083m, where you go on to Rifugio Barmasse or turn down to the empty Falegnon chalets, 1912m, and then the empty chalets of Promoron, 1796m, beside the half-way station of the Barmasse waterworks.

The path, now numbered 5 & 4, leaves from the NE corner of the security fence and in another hour drops down to the valley. When you reach a T-junction, Path No. 5 goes L to the Barmasse chalets and Path No. 4 goes R - the official AVVA No.1, turning L at the next junction down to the roadhead just NE of Valmartin, 1493m. Follow the road down into the valley bottom and just beyond the bridge over the Torrente Marmore, 50m up the other side, take a path on the L which reaches the southern outskirts of Paquier village, 1528m, the main settlement of Valtournanche.

Lignan and the Val de St. Barthélemy to Fenêtre di Tzan

Distance:	13km
Height Gain:	1101m
Height Loss:	nil

Outward		G.B.T.	Return	
		Lignan, 1633m	3hr 40	40min.
45min.	45min.	Porliod, 1867m	3hr	1hr 30
1hr 30	2hr 15	La Sayvaz, 1985m	1hr 30	50min.
1hr 30	3hr 45	Les Crotes, 2389m	40min.	40min.
1hr	4hr 45	Fenêtre di Tzan, 2734m		

The route from Lignan to the Fenêtre di Tzan is straightforward and easy. It will be used by those who have descended into the village for overnight accommodation after having used the route described in Section 3.4.

Take the road from Lignan, 1633m, via Saquignod, 1674m, and Venoz, 1755m, to the roadhead at Porliod, 1867m. From here take a path traversing across pastures to Arzech and Alpe la Noua to the restored chalets (holiday cottages?) at Chancombre, 1927m. [A road goes up from Lignan to Issologne, 1515m, and Praz, c1740m, then continues as a good track to Chancombre, but it is not so attractive as the route via Porliod as it is confined to the valley bottom]. The good track is followed all the way to La Sayvaz, 1985m, (spelt variously on signposts also as Seyvaz or Servaz).

1985m is the point of the river crossing at La Sayvaz while the farm itself is at 2001m. Here, and just up-valley to Ollière, 2007m, and the large farm of Praterier, 2060m, is a flat area of the valley floor and a fine Scots pine wood. There is a delightful climb up through the valley meadows, scattered with fallen blocks, to Les Crotes, 2389m, semi-underground byres still in good condition with stone vaulted roofs: they make good shelter.

Les Crotes is at the head of the Val de St. Barthélemy and from here there is a steep climb up zig-zags on Path No.19 to the Fenêtre di

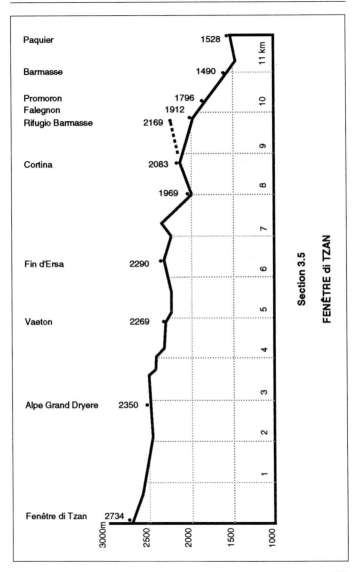

Section 3.5

FENÊTRE di TZAN

Location	Elevation
Paquier	1528
Barmasse	1490
Promoron	1796
Falegnon	1912
Rifugio Barmasse	2169
Cortina	2083
	1969
Fin d'Ersa	2290
Vaeton	2269
Alpe Grand Dryere	2350
Fenêtre di Tzan	2734

Tzan, 2734m, (local spelling: other spellings are Cian, Tsan and Tian). There is a steep final climb through scree to the ridge, rocky on the W side, grassy on the E, topped by a large wooden cross.

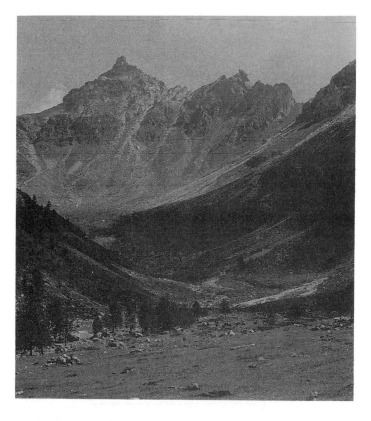

Mont Rédéssau, 3253m, and Fenêtre di Tzan, 2734m,
from Praterier, Val de Saint Barthélemy.

SECTION 3.6
COL FENÊTRE, 2182m

Distance:	10km, Lignan to Mongnod/Torgnon
Height Gain:	600m
Height Loss:	826m
Grade:	1

Outward		G.B.T.	Return	
		Lignan, 1633m	3hr 30	1hr
1hr	1hr	Praz, 1740m	2hr 30	30min.
1hr 30	2hr 30	Col Fenêtre, 2182m	2hr	2hr
1hr	3hr 30	Mongnod/Torgnon, 1489m		

This is the most frequented way from the Val de St. Barthélemy to the Valtournanche and would be particularly useful for those who have come over from the Valpelline by the Colle de Vessona. (Route 3.4). It leads from Lignan to Mongnod/Torgnon, a short and easy route, but its onward continuation to Antey St. André leaves the walker awkwardly placed for the next stage to the Valle d'Ayas, unless it be by another easy, low-level route. The route over the Colle de St. Barthélemy, Col Leché and down to Lignan, then via Porliod, Col Fenêtre and down to Antey St. André is waymarked No. 105 as a route from Aosta to Antey St. André.

The usual route is to follow the road down to Issologne, 1515m, and Praz, c1740m, but this is not as attractive as the route via Porliod, 1867m, as the former is confined to the valley bottom. (The route via Porliod entails an extra 127m of ascent and 45m of descent).

At the 1850m contour on the E(L) flank of the valley the path crosses a drainage channel which runs a distance of 10km traversing the W side of the ridge which confines the glen. It rounds the southern tip of the ridge then turns E to the village of Grand Villa, 1412m, whilst on the E side of the col, at the 1900m contour, above Chantorné, the path meets another channel that drains the Torgnon basin and which runs for a similar distance to the same destination, and at 1800m the path crosses another that is a supply for Torgnon.

The Rev. King came this way in 1855 with his mule and noted that the Col Fenêtre was also known as the Fenêtre de St. Barthélemy:

"We reached the summit of the Col ... a narrow cleft in the crest of the mountain, not many yards wide, covered with greensward and low brushwood." The descent to Torgnon *"was most delightful. After quitting the highest rocks we wound our way down among sunny glades of larches and wide prairies, like park scenes on an Alpine scale."*

Path 79 descends through Septumian, 1673m, to Mongnod, the principal settlement that makes up the scattered village of Torgnon, 1489m. The sparsely populated commune of Torgnon is spread over the long and sloping alp in splendid isolation above the Marmore torrent in the Valtournanche. The parish church dates from the 12thC but the present building dates from the second half of the last century.

There is accommodation available in Torgnon and it is only an hour for the descent on Path 63, part of the Grande Balconata, to Antey St. André, 1074m, and the main valley road up to Paquier and Cervinia.

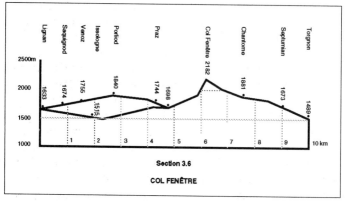

Section 3.6

COL FENÊTRE

SECTION 4
VALTOURNANCHE to VALLE d'AYAS

If the Valpelline is one of the least known valleys of the Italian
Pennine Alps then the Valtournanche is perhaps best known, if only
because it has at its head the magnificent Monte Cervino (Matterhorn)
and the ski resort of Cervinia (Breuil).

The valley enters the Valle d'Aosta at Châtillon and its neighbouring
twin St. Vincent. St. Vincent is the larger and more important of the
two. Archaeological evidence shows that St. Vincent dates from the
Roman era: in medieval times it was the home of the Montjovet and
Perron families. The fortune and fame of the place dates from the
second half of the 18thC when the Abbot Perret discovered the
therapeutic value of the waters from the springs in the hills of St.
Vincent. From that day to this the place became one of the most
celebrated curative resorts in Europe. St. Vincent is amongst the best-
known and important alpine thermal resorts. The parish church is one
of the oldest in the Valle d'Aosta, dating from the 11thC. It has a statue
of Padre Benedittini in the classic Romansch style and an interesting
crypt. There is a Romansch church in the nearby hamlet of Moron,
2km E.

Neighbouring Châtillon is at the mouth of the Valtournanche,
standing above the confluence of the Dora Baltea and the Torrente
Marmore. It is a small but busy industrial town and was important in
feudal times when the Challant and Châtillon families built their
castles in the area - the 14thC Castello di Ussel stands just across the
Dora Baltea and Châtillon's own castle was mentioned in 13thC
documents. There is a 13thC bridge over the Torrente Marmore.

Going up the Valtournanche from Châtillon you come, after 8km,
to Antey St. André, 1074m. Its position in the valley and its climate
made it a favourite home of the feudal family of Cly, who had their
summer residence here. (Their principal castle was at Chambave,

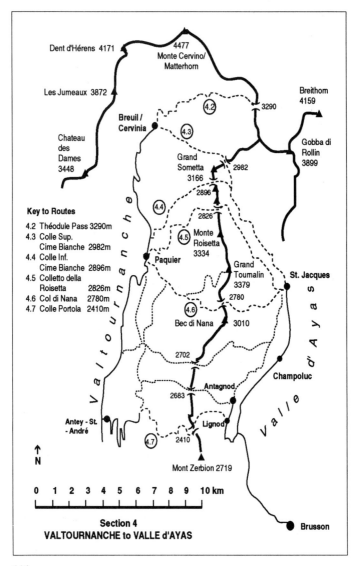

Dent d'Hérens 4171

4477
Monte Cervino/
Matterhorn

Les Jumeaux 3872

Breithorn
4159

3290

Breuil /
Cervinia

4.2

4.3

Chateau
des
Dames
3448

Gobba di
Rollin
3899

Grand
Sometta
3166

2982

2896

Key to Routes

4.2 Théodule Pass 3290m
4.3 Colle Sup.
   Cime Bianche 2982m
4.4 Colle Inf.
   Cime Bianche 2896m
4.5 Colletto della
   Roisetta   2826m
4.6 Col di Nana 2780m
4.7 Colle Portola 2410m

2826

4.4

4.5

Monte
Roisetta
3334

Paquier

Grand
Tournalin
3379

St. Jacques

2780

4.6

Bec di Nana

3010

2702

Champoluc

Antagnod

2683

Antey - St.
- André

Lignod

4.7

2410

↑
N

Mont Zerbion 2719

0   1   2   3   4   5   6   7   8   9   10 km

Section 4
VALTOURNANCHE to VALLE d'AYAS

Brusson

further up the Dora Baltea towards Aosta). The parish church dates from the 12thC but the campanile was reconstructed in the 14thC from an even earlier one. There are traces of an aqueduct dating from 1200. Ante St. André is conveniently placed for the crossing of the Col Fenêtre to the W (see 3.6) and the Colle Portola to the E (see 4.7).

Much further up the valley is the principal village of the valley, Paquier, 1528m, commonly called Valtournanche. It occupies a splendid position in mid-valley with extremely fine views down the valley, a view closed in by the distant peak of Punta Tersiva, 3512m, in the mountains of Cogne. Chestnut and walnut trees form a framework for Monte Cervino whose granite pyramid dominates the view at the head of the valley.

The 15thC parish church of St. Antoine was completely rebuilt in the second half of the last century and has a notable campanile, and is internally ornate. In the piazzetta outside the W door are tablets to the memory of Canon Jean-Antoine Carrel of Aosta, who died in 1890, aged 62, on the Cervino, and to J. Joseph Maquignaz, who also died in 1890. Local guides and mountaineers who performed heroic mountaineering feats or who died in accidents in the mountains are commemorated on numerous memorial stones, while another memorial is dedicated to those guides and mountaineers who died in the two World Wars.

The valley above Paquier can be followed by paths alongside the Torrente Marmore. On the N side of the village a short descent from the main valley road leads down to the hamlet of Crepin, 1577m, on the other side of the river. At the N end of the group of chalets Path No.20 follows the R bank of the torrent and comes, after 2km, to a deep chasm through the serpentine rock, so narrow that in some places the opposite walls almost touch each other. This spot, called the Gouffre des Busserailles, has been made accessible from below and deserves a visit.

The Gouffre des Busserailles chasm, 104m (340ft) long by 35m (115ft) deep, into which the river Marmore pours down in a 10m (33ft) drop, was first explored on 19 November 1865 by Jean-Antoine Carrel and the two Maquignaz's - J-Joseph and J-Pierre - by abseiling into the gorge. They constructed a plank gallery along its walls. In some places the torrent has wormed the rock and left natural bridges and caverns - the largest cavern is about 8.5m (28ft) in diameter and the torrent is 15m (50ft) or so below.

On the old road up the valley, now bypassed, is the little chapel of Notre Dame de la Garde. (The modern road climbs above the gorge by zig-zags and through tunnels and only a glimpse of the gorge can be seen).

At the first hairpin bend Path No.20 leaves the road to follow the river again past Albergo Carrel at Avouil, 1967m, then follows the road into Cervinia.

[Path No.20 from Paquier to Cervinia takes 2hr 30 min., plus extra time for a visit to the Gouffre. Alternatively there is a frequent 20min. bus ride, viz:

| Paquier dep. | 06.54 | 09.44 | 11.34 | 12.09 | 13.49 | 15.44 |
| Cervinia arr. | 07.15 | 10.05 | 11.55 | 12.30 | 14.10 | 16.05] |

The original alpine village of Breuil was the principal settlement at the foot of the vast glacial alp of Plan Maison, the high alpine pasture beneath Monte Cervino, now wastelands covered by ski roads and cablecars. The growth of winter sports has seen an expansion of the village by hotels and condominiums of a new tourist village which has become known as Cervinia, which is now an all-season resort. It is a styleless collection of ageing modern buildings with a half-hearted attempt at a pedestrianised main street and, as a consequence, a tortuous one-way traffic circuit. The village is not, on the whole, a place in which to linger, though it is not so crowded, expensive or tourist-ridden as Zermatt.

The oldest hotels are the Hotel du Mont Cervin and the Hotel des Jumeaux, both opened in 1865, the year in which the Cervino was first climbed. Next to the Guide's Bureau in the main street is the Museo del Cervino, with displays and artefacts relating to the history of its climbing.

The ridge of mountains that run S of the frontier ridge on the E side of the Valtournanche is not as complex as that on the W side and its summits are not quite so high or as precipitous. The range starts on the SW ridge of the extensive snow dome of the Breithorn plateau and after an initial reach to the SW it runs almost due S from the Gran Sometta, 3166m, to Mont Zerbion, 2719m, above St. Vincent in the Aosta valley.

The crossing of the ridge from Valtournanche to the Valle d'Ayas is consequently much easier and straightforward. Whether one crosses from Cervinia or Paquier to St. Jacques or Champoluc the journey should not take more than 6hr.

The NW edge of the Breithorn plateau, called Plateau Rosa, is defined on its N side by a pass at the foot of the ridge that leads up NW to the summit of the Monte Cervino/Matterhorn. This pass, the Théodule Pass, 3317m, is one of the most frequented, and in fine weather one of the easiest, glacier passes in the Alps. It is hardly surprising therefore that it has long been used as a passage from Zermatt to Cervinia and, in the present context, is used as a short circuit of Monte Rosa.

For completeness, therefore, routes out of the Valpelline to Zermatt are given in this Section and also, because of the importance of both the Théodule Pass and the Matterhorn in alpine history, sub-sections are devoted to the history of ascents of these two places: Sections 4.1 and 4.2.

There are several possible crossings of the ridge out of the Valtournanche to the Valle d'Ayas. From N to S the most practical for walkers/scramblers are:

Section	Pass	Height	Grade	Quality
4.3	Colle Sup. Cime Bianche	2982m	1	
4.4	Colle Inf. Cime Bianche	2896m	2	
4.5	Colletto della Roisetta	2826m	3	
4.6	Col di Nana	2780m	3	**
4.7	Colle Portola	2410m	1	

A scramblers' route goes up to the Passo di Tournalin, 3130m, from the Valtournanche but there is no continuation into the Valle d'Ayas.

117

The Col Pillonet, 2702m, and the Col Tantané, 2683m, have no satisfactory descents into the Valle d'Ayas.

Routes out of the Valtournanche to Zermatt are shown on LS Maps 283 Arolla and 284 Mischabel while LS 293 Valpelline and 294 Gressoney are required for all the other routes: the dividing line between the sheets follows very nearly the line of the ridge itself. All routes are shown on the IGC Sheet 5 Cervino/Matterhorn & Monte Rosa, on Kompass Sheet 87 Breuil/Cervinia-Zermatt, and on the Studio FMB Map.

From R to L: Colle Superiore delle Cime Bianche, 2982m, Colle Inferiore delle Cime Bianche, 2896m, Grand Tournalin, 3379m, Petit Tournalin, 3207m, Becca Trecare, 3033m, and Col di Nana, 2780m, from the east.

SECTION 4.1
The MATTERHORN / MONTE CERVINO, 4478m

In far off times legend says that the range of peaks which divides Italy from Switzerland was a uniform ridge instead of, as now, a series of peaks. The tale was told that Gargantua, a giant of Aosta, strode across the range with one foot on either side and as he stood here the rocks fell away and the pyramid of cliffs caught between his legs alone remained standing. Thus was the Matterhorn born.

The mountain is known by different names on either side of the frontier - Monte Cervino in Italy, Matterhorn in Switzerland - but it has had a variety of names throughout its history.

The oldest recorded name is 'Cervin' (1518) and the next after that 'Monte Silvio' (1644). For several years between 1690 and 1760 it was spelt variously as Servin, Servino and Servina. But Monte Silvio was later discovered to refer to the St. Théodule Pass and 'Silvio' had been thought of as a Latinised form of 'Cervin.' By the turn of the 17thC the peak was called 'Matter Monte' and by 1760 'Mattenberg'. In 1778 it was called 'Matter Horn alias Mons Silvius' and was at various times in the next twenty years so called. It was Horace Benedict Saussure who confirmed Matterhorn in 1798 from which date it was universally employed.

"The superstitious natives" wrote Edward Whymper *"in the surrounding valleys spoke of a ruined city on the summit wherein the spirits dwelt: and if you laughed they gravely shook their heads, told you to look yourself to see the castle and walls, and warned against a rash assault, lest the infuriated demons from their impregnable heights might hurl down vengeance for one's derision."*

The history of the successive attempts to challenge the wild man who lived on the top and to conquer this formidable peak is well-known to those interested in Alpine adventure, and has been graphically told by Whymper in his classic *Scrambles Among the Alps*.

It was Jean-Jacques Carrel of Breuil who was the first to doubt the mountain's inaccessibility. In 1858 he and two natives from the village - Jean-Antoine Carrel and a boy, Aimé Gorret - made the first attempt and reached the Tête du Lion, 3715m, and this spurred other attempts, principally by Edward Whymper.

Edward Whymper was the son of a wood engraver. He was taken away from school at the age of 14 and was apprenticed to his father's business. His work attracted the attention of William Longman, the publisher, who was in need of illustrations for a book on the Alps, and who commissioned Whymper to produce the illustrations.

Whymper was 20 when he went to the Alps in 1860 and first saw the Matterhorn and in 1861 he returned to make his first attempt on the peak from the Italian side, following the route of 1858. It was from Breuil that his seven unsuccessful attempts were launched (1861-65).

In 1862 Whymper reached a point higher than anyone before him - 4115m (13,500ft) - and in 1863 he had the satisfaction of seeing Prof. John Tyndall (the famous scientist and conqueror of the Weisshorn in 1861) with the two Carrels fail shortly after reaching the minor summit which still bears his name - Pic Tyndall, 4241m.

In the same year, 1863, some leading mountaineers, among them two distinguished scientists, Felice Giordano and Quintino Sella, founded the Italian Alpine Club (CAI) in Turin. They resolved that it should be the Italians who should have the honour of making the first ascent of the Matterhorn.

Whymper knew nothing of these plans when he arrived in Breuil on 8 July 1865 hoping to persuade J.A.Carrel to join him in an attack on the E face. But Carrel had been engaged by "an Italian family" (who happened to be Giordano and Sella) so Whymper decided to cross the Théodule Pass to Zermatt and engage the first competent guide that he could find there for an attack on the Swiss side. But at Breuil Whymper met Lord Francis Douglas (who had just made the second ascent of the Obergabelhorn, 4063m, with Peter Taugwalder, only a day after its first ascent, but the first ascent from Zinal) who had also hoped to engage Carrel. Finding Carrel unavailable both

Whymper and Douglas crossed to Zermatt on 12 July where they found the Rev. Charles Hudson and 19 year old Douglas Hadow. Hudson was proposing to attempt the Matterhorn with Michel Croz, a great Chamonix guide, and the two Taugwalders (Peter, father and son) from Zermatt.

It was readily agreed that it would be undesirable for two parties to be on the mountain at the same time and that it was essential to join forces. (It had been said that, such was Whymper's obsession to win the race for the Matterhorn that he 'muscled in' on Hudson's party, wanting to get up the mountain before Carrel's 'Italian family').

Whymper's party left Zermatt on 13 July and camped at 3350m (11,000ft) and on the next day, at 13.40, reached the summit. On the descent, a little below the summit, at 3.15 in the afternoon (indicated by a watch discovered on Hadow's body) Hadow slipped, pushed over Croz and pulled over Hudson and Douglas, and the rope broke between Douglas and Taugwalder. Hadow, Douglas, Hudson and Croz all fell to their deaths. Whymper and the two Taugwalders alone survived. They spent a miserable night on the E face and on the following day descended to Zermatt.

On 17 July 1865 - three days after Whymper's ascent - the first ascent was made from the Italian side by Jean-Antoine Carrel and Jean-Baptiste Bich. Carrel died 35 years later in September 1900 on the Italian ridge which he had been the first to conquer. He suddenly collapsed and died on easy ground after a descent from a storm. He was 62.

The first lady to reach the summit was Félicité Carrel of Valtournanche on 13 September 1867 via the Italian Ridge. The Col Félicité at 4380m is named after her.

The mountain has been the subject of several record attempts. Viktor Kronig, former Swiss world ski champion, reached the summit in 4hr after leaving the church in Zermatt in 1955: the altitude difference is 2861m.

The north faces of the three giants of the Alps - Eiger, Grandes Jorasses and Matterhorn - were first climbed in 1978 by Yvano Ghiradina, solo and in winter. Christophe Profit made successful record ascents of the trio in summer 1985 (24hr) then in winter 1987 (41hr) while in 1981 Jean-Marc Boivin skied down the E face of the Matterhorn, climbed its N face then descended from the summit by hang glider.

The Italian or West Summit, 4476m, is c60 metres from the Swiss or East Summit, 4478m. On the Italian peak is a 3m high steel cross, erected in 1902. On the Swiss peak is a statue of St. Bernard, erected on the 125th anniversary of Whymper's ascent. The anniversary in 1990 was a week of celebrations in Zermatt and Cervinia: on 14 July 1990 an Anglo-French-Swiss team of seven mountaineers - whose combined ages totalled 125 years - climbed the original route and for the first time in its history the mountain was closed for the day to all non-official parties.

Monte Cervino, 4478m, and the Dent d'Hérens, 4171m,
from near Cheneil, 2105m.

SECTION 4.2
The (ST.) THÉODULE PASS
(Colle de Teodulo), 3290m

The Ascent

It is perhaps doubtful if many people today make a crossing of the Théodule Pass from Cervinia to Zermatt on foot as mechanical transport reaches up from both the Italian and Swiss sides. That on the Italian side is by cable car from Cervinia via Plan Maison to the Testa Grigia, 3480m, requiring a descent N down a narrow snow ridge for 1km to the pass. A combination of cable cars, gondolas and chairlifts bring the tourists up from Zermatt via Furi, Furgg and Trockenerstegg direct to the pass.

Outward		G.B.T.	Return	
		Cervinia, 2006m	6hr	30min.
1hr 30	1hr 30	Plan Maison, 2547m	5hr 30	1hr 30
2hr 30	4hr	Colle de Teodulo, 3290m	4hr	1hr
1hr	5hr	Gandegghutte, 3029m	3hr	3hr
2hr	7hr	Zermatt, 1616m		

The classic route of ascent from Cervinia is from the Albergo Piovano al Giomein on Path No.25 past La Veille, crossing a stream and across grassy slopes to Tramail la Veille, 2447m, and the Albergo Plan Maison, 2547m. From this cable car transfer station take a path which goes NE in the direction of a ski lift. The path runs easterly alongside a ski tow and reaches the Capanna Bontadini, 3055m, a useful emergency shelter. Continue slightly S of E, traversing the glacier slope to reach the pass.

The short bit of glacier on the Italian side is easy. The larger glacier on the Swiss side is also quite easy but large concealed crevasses often occur: parties are advised to be roped. The crossing is easy, though it is laborious after a fall of snow. There is usually a well-defined track over it.

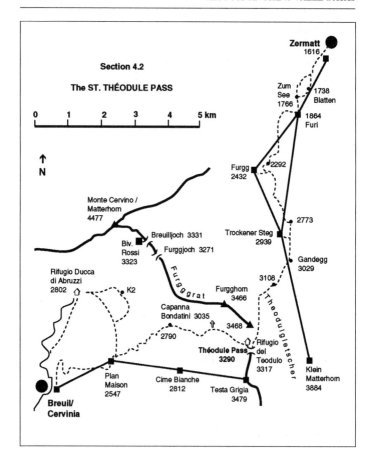

Section 4.2

The ST. THÉODULE PASS

The Hut

Five minutes' ascent from the snow up screes to the NW is the CAI
Rifugio Teodulo/Theodul Hutte, 3317m. On this spot H.B. de
Saussure spent three days (11-14 August) in 1792 in a temporary
shed, making, during his stay, scientific observations and making the
first ascent (on 13 August) of the Klein Matterhorn, 3884m (or, as he

called it, the Cime Brune du Breithorn). Saussure called the pass the
'Col du Mont Cervin' and the ruins of the hut he built were found later
by several travellers. They were still there in 1830 when the Earl of
Minto used them as a bivouac. Then in 1851 a hut was being built just
above the pass by J. P. Meynet of Valtournanche, nephew of the J. J.
Meynet whom Saussure met in 1792. Sir Alfred Wills saw it being
constructed when he came this way on 14 September 1852. The hut
was completed in 1854 and was occupied by Hinchliff, then in 1855
by the Rev. S. W. King and his wife. The Meynets sold the hut in 1860
to a group of men of Valtournanche who, in 1864, completed the
wooden 'annexe', then the hut was taken over by the Italian Alpine
Club. The present hut was built in 1920. It has 86 beds and is open
from 1 April to 30 September.

The View
The view from the pass, or the hut, is extensive. To the SW countless
Alps stretch away in magnificent ranges to the Gran Paradiso, the La
Grivola, 3969m, and the Testa del Rutor, 3485m, being the most
prominent mountains in the distance. Nearer, in the same direction,
are the crests passed in the previous four days, the chief peaks visible
being the Bec de Luseney and Dent d'Hérens. Eastward, over the
wide sloping glacier leading down to Zermatt, magnificent mounded
cliffs of névé rise to the sheeted ice mass of the Klein Matterhorn. To
the L of it, a little to the rear, is the grandly shaped cone of the
Breithorn, 4164m, its summit an oval point of exquisitely pure
unsullied white, almost too dazzling to look at. Monte Rosa is just
concealed behind the Breithorn, but the vast Gorner Glacier, rolling
down from its northern side, from the Liskamm, 4479m, comes into
sight, sweeping round the cliffs of the Hohtälliigrat, Gornergrat,
Riffelhorn and Riffelberg.

"But the most wonderful feature of all" wrote the Rev. King " - *and
one which neither eye nor mind can at first fully grasp - is the
stupendous mass of the Cervin, rising, a solid obelisk of utterly
inaccessible rock* (as indeed it was in 1855) *8000 feet high about its
glacier beds, and much of it far too precipitous for snow to rest on it*

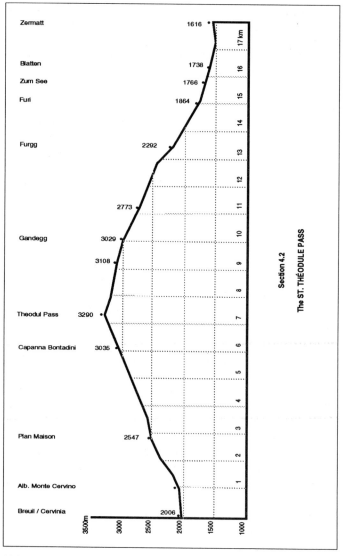

Section 4.2

The ST. THÉODULE PASS

for any length of time." The Matterhorn looks gigantic from this view. One sees 'The Shoulder' and the notch between it and the final peak which stopped Tyndall, 'The Great Tower', the Tête and the Col du Lion. The Theodulhorn, 3469m, comes in front of it, and it can be easily ascended from the pass.

History

The Théodule Pass is one of the oldest routes out of the Vale d'Aosta but there is no evidence that it was known to the Romans. The first distinct mention of it was in 1528 when it was called 'Mons Gletscher' by the famous Swiss historian Aegidius Tschudi (1505-72).

W. A. B. Coolidge, in his *Alpine Studies,* 1912, had discovered the use of five names by other topographers between 1528 and 1598. The Valaisans called it 'Der Gletscher' while the inhabitants of Aosta called it 'Mont Rosa'. The word 'ruize', 'roise', 'roësa' or 'rosa' is the local Aostan patois name for a glacier, so that the Aostan name 'Rosa' is a simple translation of the name 'Der Gletscher' given by the Valaisans. Later the term 'Rosa' shifted towards the E and became specially attached to the highest point of 'The Glacier', namely Monte Rosa. 'Mons', becoming 'Mont' and 'Monte', was the 16thC word for a pass, not of a peak. Other names during the mid-late 16thC were 'Mons Sylvius', 'Augstalerberg' and 'Mons Matter' by topographers such as Johannes Stumpf in 1548 (1500-1566), Sebastian Münster in 1550 and Josias Simler in 1574.

In a map of 1620 'M. della Roisa' had been moved further E, to an area between the Lys and Sesia valleys, and really seems to mean Monte Rosa, while various maps between 1630 and 1690 gave 'Monte Silvio', 'Mte Silvio' or 'M. Silvio' to the Matterhorn. The other names began to fall out of use by the third quarter of the century.

But in 1683 Tommaso Borgonio published a great map (dated 1680) of the Dominions of the Duke of Savoy in which the fortifications of the 'St. Théodelle' are associated with this pass. (By a striking coincidence the name 'M. Servino' appears on this map for the Matterhorn, but it was not until the 1790s that 'Mont Cervin' or 'M. Cervino' appeared).

In about 1688 a great wooden statue of St. Théodule was erected on the pass. St. Théodule was the first bishop of Sion and the patron saint of the Valais. The fortifications on the pass came about because of the necessity of the Duke of Savoy to close all approaches to his territory to the banished Waldensians from re-entering their native valleys in Italy, from where they had been driven out in 1687. (You will recall the fortification ruins on the Fenêtre de Durand). However, in 1689 the Waldensians returned to the valley of Aosta by crossing the Col du Bonhomme, the Col du Mont Iseran, the Little Mont Cenis and the Col de Clapier.

When P. A. Arnod, a high official of the Duchy of Aosta, wrote his report in 1694 of the then-known passes round the valley of Aosta, he wrote of the *"old and rude wooden statue called St. Théodule on the summit of the pass."*

By the 1730s-40s 'Mons Matter' became 'Mons Matten' and by 1760 became 'Mattenberg'. Mattenberg referred to the ridge over which the pass 'Silvius' lay. By 1778 'Mattenberg' became 'Mattenhorn' and shifted from the ridge of the pass to the peak above it.

Up till now no definite passage of the pass had been mentioned since that by Tschudi in 1528. But two or three crossings took place between 1758 and 1764 by father and son, Peter and Thomas Abraham, collectors employed by the celebrated Swiss botanist Albrecht von Haller, who was Director of the salt mine at Bex in those years (i.e. 1758-64). Abraham and Haller both called the pass 'Mons Sylvius'.

The existence of the pass was revealed to the outside world at large by H. B. de Saussure who crossed it on 14 August 1789 from Breuil to Zermatt and he spent three days there exactly three years later. Saussure's accounts of 1789 and 1792 were not published until 1796 but in July 1795 the botanist Thomas Abraham made another crossing of the pass, which he still called 'Mont Silvio', reserving the name St. Théodule for the 17thC fortifications. The peak to the W he called the Matterhorn, a derivation of its 1778 name.

St. Théodule was the name still reserved for the fortifications in 1820 and the pass was given 'Matterjoch' and 'Col de Cervin' and it

Above: The Monte Rosa group, Rothorn and Testa Grigia from the Canale di Saint Vincent, Val d'Ayas   *Below:* Castor, Pollux, Lyskam, Dufourspitze, Pyramide Vincent and Monte Rosa dominate the head of the Val d'Ayas

Pollux, Castor, and Lyskam from the Col d'Olen, 2881m
Rifugio Ospizio Sottile, 2480m, on the Colle Valdobbia

was not until the 1840s that new map-makers gave it the name by which it is known today - the St. Théodule Pass.

English visitors to or across the pass were several in the early years of alpine exploration. These were:

1821 or 1822	the celebrated astronomer Sir John Herschel, en route to the Breithorn
1825	William Brockenden (*Journals of Excursions in the Alps,* 1833)
1825	Messrs. Frank and Horace Walker
1830	Earl of Minto
1840	A. T. Malkin
1840	John Ball
September 1841	J. D. Forbes
26 August 1842	J. D. Forbes and Bernard Studer
1849	John Ruskin
14 September 1852	Sir Alfred Wills and party, from Zermatt to Châtillon (*Wanderings Among the High Alps,* 1856)
27 July 1853	F. F. Tuckett and J. H. Fox
2 September 1853	John Ball
1854	T. W. Hinchliff (*Summer Months Among the Alps,* 1857)
1855	Rev. S. W. King (*The Italian Valleys of the Pennine Alps,* 1858)
26 June 1856	F. F. Tuckett and J. H. Fox

Tuckett's account of his 1856 crossing is typical of the work done by these alpine explorers. They left Zermatt at 1.30am in *"most exquisite moonlight"*, reached the snow *"at 4.30 a.m. soon after the sun rose"* and *"at 6.30 reached the summit at a splendid pace, having probably made one of the quickest passes on record."* They stayed an hour in the *"very comfortable shelter (of) a chalet which has recently been erected there, the floor of which was one mass of ice, whilst icicles hung from the rafters, and the walls were covered with the most beautiful frost limitations."* At 7.30 they started their descent but instead of taking the 'ordinary' route to Valtournanche they crossed the snows to the Colle Superiore delle Cime Bianche, down to St. Jacques in the Val d'Ayas, where at 1 pm they lay down to rest and doze. After *"three most delightful dreamy hours"* they set off again and at 7pm reached their *"homely but comfortable quarters"* at Brusson *"after one of the hardest day's work we had yet had."* - an 18hr day!

Monte Cervino, 4478m, from the Grande Balconata near Cheneil, 2105m.

COLLE SUPERIORE delle CIME BIANCHE, 2982m

Distance: 13.5km, Cervinia to St. Jacques
Height Gain: 976m
Height Loss: 1293m
Grade: 1

Outward		G.B.T.	Return	
		Breuil/Cervinia, 2006m	7hr	1hr
1hr 30	1hr 30	Plan Maison, 2547m	6hr	1hr
1hr 20	2hr 50	Lago Goillet, 2516m	5hr	1hr
1hr 05	3hr 55	Colle Superiore, 2982m	4hr	1hr 30
1hr 20	5hr 15	Alpe Masse, 2400m	2hr 30	1hr 30
1hr 20	6hr 35	Fiery, 1878m	1hr	1hr
50min.	7hr 25	St. Jacques, 1689m		

The route from Breuil/Cervinia to the pass is easy but uninspiring, except for the backwards views which are the only advantage. An ascent may be made of the Gran Sometta, 3166m. The descent to St. Jacques is ample compensation for the dull ascent.

From Cervinia there is a choice of three routes to the pass:

4.3.1   From the gondola station take Path No.22 all the way to the pass, passing La Suche, 2226m, and go S of Lago Goillet, 2516m. The route is scarred by pistes and for the most part follows a dirt road. A good stiff walk, but a boring one.

4.3.2   Take the gondola from Cervinia to Plan Maison, 2547m, then transfer to the cable car that goes to Plateau Rosa (Testa Grigia), 3480m. (Not to be confused with the more exciting Testa Grigia, between Champoluc and Gressoney: see Section 5.3). Get off at the midway station called Stazione Cime Bianche, 2814m. No facilities here. Allow 1hr waiting for gondolas/cablecars from Cervinia to arrive and transfer you to this point. The fare is the same price as if you are going all the way up to Plateau Rosa.

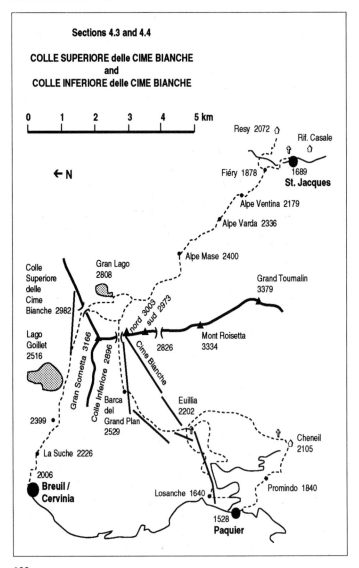

Sections 4.3 and 4.4

COLLE SUPERIORE delle CIME BIANCHE
and
COLLE INFERIORE delle CIME BIANCHE

0   1   2   3   4   5 km

← N

Resy 2072

Rif. Casale

Fiéry 1878

1689
St. Jacques

Alpe Ventina 2179

Alpe Varda 2336

Alpe Mase 2400

Gran Lago
2808

Colle
Superiore
delle
Cime
Bianche 2982

Grand Tournalin
3379

nord 3003 sud 2973

Lago
Goillet
2516

Gran Sometta 3166

Colle Inferiore 2896

Cime Bianche

2826

Mont Roisetta
3334

2399

Barca
del
Grand Plan
2529

Euillia
2202

Cheneil
2105

La Suche 2226

2006
Breuil /
Cervinia

Losanche 1640

Promindo 1840

1528
Paquier

From cablecar Stazione Cime Bianche go S on a dirt road, Path No.24, on W side of Lago Cime Bianche, 2808m, passing Capanna Gaspard, c2840m, after 30min. and reach the pass in another 30min. (though signposts say 1hr 30min. from the Stazione to the pass).

The route is scarred by a constructor's dirt road all the way through a desolate bowl of glacial debris. A new chairlift system for skiers has been constructed up to the ridge N of Colle Sup. Cime Bianche and may now be open to take summer walkers to this point.

4.3.3   From Plan Maison, 2547m, Path No.23, becoming Path 37 goes round the N and E sides of Lago Goillet, 2516m. Join Path 22 at c2600m and follow it to the pass.

Ascent of Gran Sometta, 3166m

From the Colle it is an easy ascent up the NE ridge for 1hr to the summit. It is notable for the good backward view of Cervinia, hemmed in by the stupendous cliffs of the Grandes Murailles, 3904m, Les Jumeaux, 3872m, Dent d'Hérens, 4171m, and Monte Cervino, 4477m, and for the forward view of the Breithorn-Gobba di Rollin snow dome.

The Colle is marked by a signpost at a junction of dirt roads. There is slightly higher ground to the SE on which there are several cairns: the path goes N of these. (There could be confusion here in mist/cloud as the path is faint and there are several rocky outcrops and many snow patches to avoid). Pick up the main path, No.6, down to the outlet of the icy Gran Lago, 2808m.

(If you trend too far S of Colle Superiore you go down a trough below chairlifts on Path No.1 to join the Colle Inferiore route. If so, turn L at the first small tarn and follow the stream to reach the Gran Lago path. If, instead of turning L at the first tarn, you turn L at the second, larger tarn, Lago Pesso, and follow its outlet stream you end up going down the Cortoz glen. This is not a very interesting route but it is a useful escape in bad weather or an emergency down a jeep

133

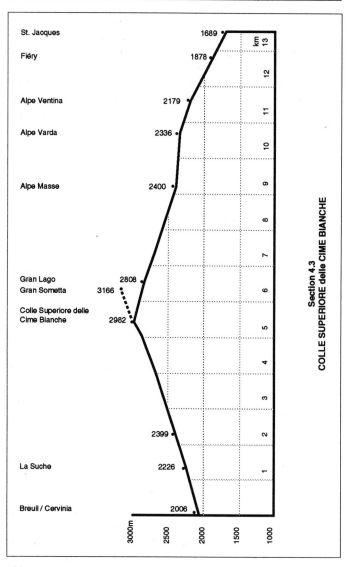

Section 4.3
COLLE SUPERIORE delle CIME BIANCHE

St. Jacques — 1689 — km 13
Fiéry — 1878
Alpe Ventina — 2179
Alpe Varda — 2336
Alpe Masse — 2400
Gran Lago — 2808
Gran Sometta — 3166
Colle Superiore delle Cime Bianche — 2982
La Suche — 2226
2399
Breuil / Cervinia — 2006

track making a gradual descending traverse on the valley side to St. Jacques).

The Grand Lago path is through lovely scenery. There is a steep descent over the 2000m contour to the level of the Conca di Rollin combe below the ice cap of the Gobba di Rollin/Breithorn dome. Cross the stream several times on the way to Alpe Masse, 2400m, superbly sited among glacial debris and boulders in a wild and barren landscape. A view extends down the valley SE over St. Jacques (unseen) to the Testa Grigia, 3315m, directly ahead. The path keeps to the stream, crossing and recrossing, past the ruins of Alpe Varda, 2336m, then there is a steep descent past Alpe Ventina, 2179m, and through woods to Fiéry, 1878m.

Fiéry no longer provides accommodation as shown on some maps. (It used to be the Albergo Bela Vista). For accommodation you can either descend to St. Jacques or traverse to Resy, 2072m.

[For Resy, go up Path No. 7 a short way and pass in front of the six-storey former Casa Alpina Bosco beside its huge boulder. Follow Path No. 8A down to cross the Torrente di Verra stream by a bridge and go up the other side to join a rough track. Go up the zig-zag track then traverse R on Path No. 8B for a fairly level approach to Resy, 2072m. (If you go down the track then go L on Path No. 8A to Rascard, 1865m, there is still a stiff climb up through woods to Resy). There are two private and popular rifugios at Resy - Rifugio Ferraro and Rifugio dell Guide Frachey - both converted out of old farm buildings. They command a superb view down the valley and across to the Grand Tournalin, 3379m].

From Fiéry pass between the old hotel and the chapel, turn L and go down a steep cobbled path - take care, smooth and slippery, especially when wet, though much eroded in the upper reaches - to Blanchard where you cross the Torrent di Verra to reach a road. At the next (road) bridge 100 metres downstream notice that the Torrente di Verra is joined by the clearer waters of the Torrente Cortoz flowing under a massive split boulder. The road soon leads into the village of St. Jacques, 1689m.

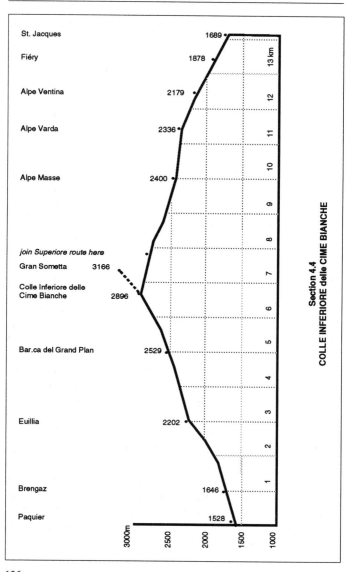

St. Jacques — 1689
Fiéry — 1878
Alpe Ventina — 2179
Alpe Varda — 2336
Alpe Masse — 2400

join Superiore route here
Gran Sometta — 3166
Colle Inferiore delle Cime Bianche — 2896
Bar.ca del Grand Plan — 2529
Euillia — 2202
Brengaz — 1646
Paquier — 1528

Section 4.4
COLLE INFERIORE delle CIME BIANCHE

SECTION 4.4
COLLE INFERIORE delle CIME BIANCHE, 2896m

Distance:	14.2km, Paquier to St. Jacques		
Height Gain:	1368m		
Height Loss:	1207m		
Grade:	2		

Outward		G.B.T.	Return	
		Paquier, 1528m	6hr	30min.
30min.	30min.	Losanche, 1640m	5hr 30	1hr
2hr	2hr 30	Euillia, 2202m	4hr 30	30min.
30min.	3hr	Bar. del Gran Plan, 2529m	4hr	30min.
1hr	4hr	Colle Inferiore, 2896m	3hr 30	1hr
1hr	5hr	Alpe Masse, 2400m	2hr 30	1hr 30
1hr 20	6hr 20	Fiéry, 1878m	1hr	1hr
50min.	7hr 10	St. Jacques, 1689m		

This route passes S of the Gran Sometta, 3166m, and also enables an ascent of that peak, but its disadvantage is that it does not have such magnificent backwards views as that to the N. It is also scarred by dirt roads and pistes and chairlift systems but the route is not so desolate as that of the route to the Colle Superiore. The descent to St. Jacques is almost the same as that from the Colle Superiore, but a start is more conveniently made from Paquier than from Cervinia.

From Paquier walk up the valley past the cemetery towards Cervinia. The path, No. 20, starts 700 metres N of Paquier at the road sign of the hamlet of Tourtourusa and climbs up to the school and chapel at Losanche, 1640m. At the water supply near the chapel climb up steeply between meadows to Pessey, 1788m, and an exchange station for the Losanche-Euillia 'Cime Bianche' gondolas. Keep the stream on your L then cross it by a rustic bridge then climb a delightful zig-zag path up to Euillia, 2202m, (also spelt Euillaz and Ollia).

Ascent of Gran Sometta, 3166m
From the Colle it is a comfortable ascent up the S
ridge for 1hr to the summit. It is notable for the good
backward view of Cervinia, hemmed in by the
stupendous cliffs of the Grandes Murailles, 3904m,
Les Jumeaux, 3872m, Dent d'Hérens, 4171m, and
Monte Cervino, 4477m, and for the forward view of
the Breithorn-Gobba di Rollin snow dome.

[Alternatively go further up the main valley road and take the
'Cime Bianche' gondola all the way to Euillia. It keeps close company
with Path No. 20.] The path emerges beside an active little farm
beside the square chapel of Notre Dame de la Salette, 2202m, built
in 1860.

From the chapel pass under the cables of a ski tow and continue on
Path No. 20 to the stone barns of Alpe Euillia Perron, 2380m, (water).
Traverse round to join a ski road just above the bottom station of the
Becca d'Aran chairlift and turn diagonally L up the ski road. Follow
the road past the end of a ski tow and a fenced-in pond (water supply
for snow-making canon) and continue on the road to the new farm
(1980) of Baracca del Grand Plan, 2529m. Go straight up the valley
eastwards to the pass, also called Colle Sud, a narrow pass occupied
by chairlift pylons.

On the far side of the Colle descend to the bottom of the chairlift
system down snow or scree. The valley trough on the L comes down
from the Colle Superiore. Traverse SE on Path No. 6B following the
outlet stream from a small tarn on the L , picking up Path No. 6A from
the Colletto della Roisetta, 2826m, to join Path No. 6 and AVVA No.
3 coming down from Gran Lago.

[Alternatively, if you turn R at the bottom of the chairlift system
you come to a second, larger tarn, Lago Pesso, 2825m. If you follow
its outlet stream you end up going down the Cortoz glen. This is not
a very interesting route but it is a useful escape in bad weather or an

emergency down a jeep track making a gradual descending traverse on the valley side to St. Jacques].

The Grand Lago path is through lovely scenery. There is a steep descent over the 2000m contour to the level of the Conca di Rollin combe below the ice cap of the Gobba di Rollin/Breithorn dome. Cross the stream several times on the way to Alpe Masse, 2400m, superbly sited among glacial debris and boulders in a wild and barren landscape. A view extends down the valley SE over St. Jacques (unseen) to the Testa Grigia, 3315m, directly ahead. The path keeps to the stream, crossing and recrossing, past the ruins of Alpe Varda, 2336m, then there is a steep descent past Alpe Ventina, 2179m, and through woods to Fiéry, 1878m.

Fiéry no longer provides accommodation as shown on some maps. (It used to be the Albergo Bela Vista). For accommodation you can either descend to St. Jacques or traverse to Resy, 2072m.

[For Resy, go up Path No. 7 a short way and pass in front of the six-storey former Casa Alpina Bosco beside its huge boulder. Follow Path No. 8A down to cross the Torrente diVerra stream by a bridge and go up the other side to join a rough track. Go up the zig-zag track then traverse R on Path No. 8B for a fairly level approach to Resy, 2072m. (If you go down the track then go L on Path No. 8A to Rascard, 1865m, there is still a stiff climb up through woods to Resy). There are two private and popular rifugios at Resy - Rifugio Ferraro and Rifugio dell Guide Frachey - both converted out of old farm buildings. They command a superb view down the valley and across to the Grand Tournalin, 3379m].

From Fiéry pass between the old hotel and the chapel, turn L and go down a steep cobbled path - take care, smooth and slippery, especially when wet, though much eroded in the upper reaches - to Blanchard where you cross the Torrent di Verra to reach a road. At the next (road) bridge 100 metres downstream notice that the Torrente di Verra is joined by the clearer waters of the Torrente Cortoz flowing under a massive split boulder. The road soon leads into the village of St. Jacques, 1689m.

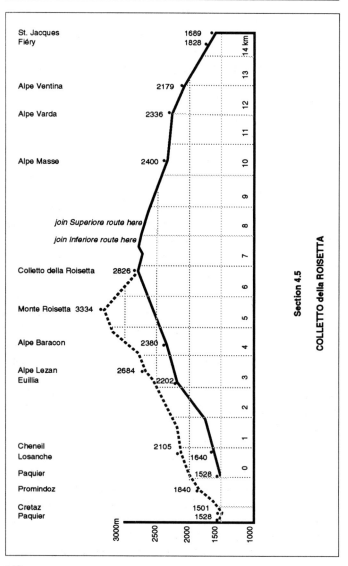

St. Jacques 1689
Fiéry 1828

Alpe Ventina 2179

Alpe Varda 2336

Alpe Masse 2400

join Superiore route here

join Inferiore route here

Colletto della Roisetta 2826

Monte Roisetta 3334

Alpe Baracon 2380

Alpe Lezan 2684
Euillia 2202

Cheneil 2105
Losanche 1640

Paquier 1528

Promindoz 1840

Cretaz 1501
Paquier 1528

Section 4.5

COLLETTO della ROISETTA

SECTION 4.5
COLLETTO della ROISETTA, 2826m

Distance:	14.7km, Paquier to St. Jacques
Height Gain:	1298m
Height Loss:	1137m
Grade:	3

Outward		G.B.T.	Return	
		Paquier, 1528m	6hr 30	30min.
30min.	30min.	Losanche, 1640m	6hr	1hr
2hr	2hr 30	Euillia, 2202m	5hr	1hr 30
1hr 30	4hr	Colletto Roisetta, 2826m	3hr 30	1hr
1hr	5hr	Alpe Masse, 2400m	2hr 30	1hr 30
1hr 20	5hr 20	Fiéry, 1828m	1hr	1hr
50min.	6hr 10	St. Jacques, 1689m		

The Cime Bianche with its twin tops, Bec Carre, 3004m, and Punta Sud, 2973m, stands between this pass and the Colle Inferiore delle Cime Bianche and is sometimes called the Bochetta Sud del Colle Inferiore dell Cime Bianche, which is a bit of a mouthful. The other name, Colle della Punta Sud, isn't very imaginative either. The ascent and descent to the Valle d'Ayas is very similar to Route 4.4 but it involves slightly less effort and is not so scarred by skiing developments.

From Paquier walk up the main valley road towards Cervinia. The path, No. 20, starts 700 metres N of Paquier at the road sign of the hamlet of Tourtourusa and climbs up to the school and chapel at Losanche, 1640m. At the water supply near the chapel climb up steeply between meadows to Pessey, 1788m, and an exchange station for the Losanche-Euillia 'Cime Bianche' gondolas. Keep the stream on your L then cross it by a rustic bridge then climb a delightful zig-zag path up to Euillia, 2202m (also spelt Euillaz and Ollia).

[Alternatively go further up the main valley road and take the 'Cime Bianche' gondola all the way to Euilla. It keeps close company with Path No. 20]. The path emerges beside an active little farm beside the square chapel of Notre Dame de la Salette, 2202m, built in 1860.

From the chapel pass under the cables of a ski tow and continue on Path No. 20 to the stone barns of Alpe Euillia Perron, 2380m, (water). Traverse round to join a ski road just above the bottom station of the Becca d'Aran chairlift and turn diagonally L up the ski road then soon turn R on another ski road, now Path No. 21, following generally the line of the chairlift to Alpe Baracon, 2380m. A second chairlift goes up NE to Cime Bianche itself but our path goes more generally E, climbing finally to the Colletto.

From the Colletto descend NE on Path No. 6A to the path descending the Cortoz glen. [Alternatively cross over the stream to join the Gran Lago path for the more interesting Section 4.4 descent to St. Jacques]. Just before this path crosses the stream coming down from Lago Verde, 2723m, on the eastern flank of the Grand Tournalin, 3379m, at about 2100m, a man-made watercourse picks up water from the Torrente Cortoz and we follow it, soon on a jeep track, Path No. 5. The watercourse is the Canale di St. Vincent, a massive aqueduct (also called the Canale Cortoz) carrying the water for 25km along the flanks of the Ayas valley to the Font de Napoleon on the Colle di Joux at 1640m, where it is then fed to St. Vincent. It took 40 years to dig at the end of the 14thC by the abbots of Emarese, St. Vincent and Challant St. Anselme, who had obtained in 1393 from the Ibleto of Challant authority to take water from the Ventina Glacier to irrigate their fields.

Leave the Canale and Path No. 5 and follow the road down to the crossing of the Torrente Cortox at Blanchard, where it flows under a massive split boulder to join the muddier waters of the Torrente di Verra. Follow the road down and you are soon in St. Jacques, 1689m.

SECTION 4.6
COL di NANA, 2780m

Distance:	**12.3km, Paquier to St. Jacques**	
Height Gain:	**1327m**	
Height Loss:	**1166m**	
Grade:	**3****	

Outward		G.B.T.	Return	
		Paquier, 1528m	6hr 15	30min.
1hr	1hr	Promindo, 1804m	5hr 45	15min.
45min.	1hr 45	Cheneil, 2105m	5hr 30	1hr
1hr 30	3hr 15	Pso del Fontanette, 2697m	4hr 30	45min.
1hr	4hr 15	Col di Nana, 2780m	3hr 45	20min.
20min.	4hr 35	Alpe Tournalin, 2534m	3hr 25	3hr 25
2hr 40	7hr 15	St. Jacques, 1689m		

From the Cretaz hamlet on the S side of Paquier the AVVA No.1 is followed all the way to the pass and is well-used as a consequence. The path was formerly numbered Path No. 2, but it is now No. 25 to Cheneil and No. 24A from Cheneil to the pass. It is a shorter route than Sections 4.3, 4.4 and 4.5 though it has two steep but easy climbs - first up through the trees to Cheneil and then up to the Passo del Fontanette - and is full of interest throughout.

As a bonus ascents can be made of a number of peaks on the main dividing ridge and there is good accommodation at the Albergo Panorama at Cheneil. It would be well worth spending two nights at Cheneil to climb one or more of these peaks on a 'rest' day.

From Cretaz the path zig-zags up through woods to the modernised and preserved Promindo chalets, 1804m, (water) and emerges above the treeline at Cheneil, 2105m. [This point can also be reached by road via Brengaz in the same time: the road stops short of the stream that runs through the alp. You can also get to Cheneil from Cervinia on Path No.107 - part of the Grande Balconata - in 3hr 30min.].

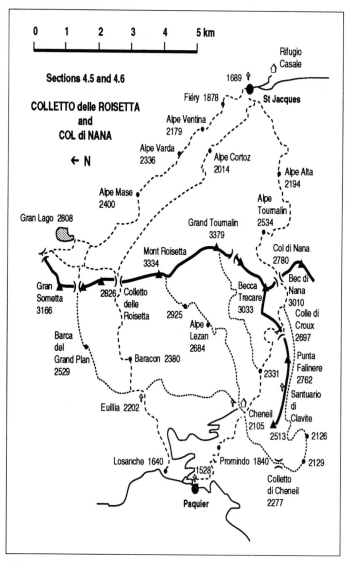

0 1 2 3 4 5 km

Sections 4.5 and 4.6

COLLETTO delle ROISETTA
and
COL di NANA

← N

Rifugio Casale
1689
St Jacques
Fiéry 1878
Alpe Ventina 2179
Alpe Varda 2336
Alpe Cortoz 2014
Alpe Alta 2194
Alpe Mase 2400
Alpe Tournalin 2534
Gran Lago 2808
Grand Tournalin 3379
Col di Nana 2780
Mont Roisetta 3334
Becca Trecare 3033
Bec di Nana 3010
Gran Sometta 3166
2826
Colletto delle Roisetta
Colle di Croux 2697
2925
Alpe Lezan 2684
Barca del Grand Plan 2529
Baracon 2380
Punta Falinere 2762
2331
Santuario di Clavite
Euillia 2202
Cheneil 2105
2513
2126
Losanche 1640
Promindo 1840
2129
1528
Colletto di Cheneil 2277
Paquier

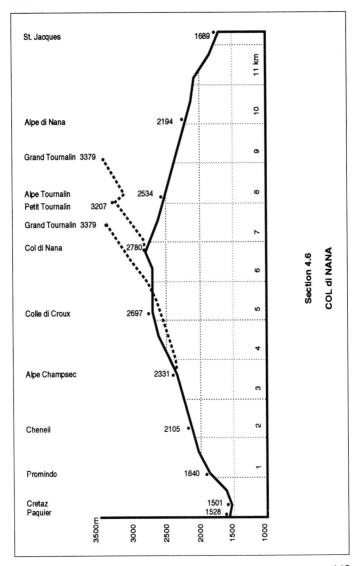

St. Jacques — 1689

Alpe di Nana — 2194

Grand Tournalin 3379

Alpe Tournalin — 2534
Petit Tournalin 3207

Grand Tournalin 3379

Col di Nana — 2780

Colle di Croux — 2697

Alpe Champsec — 2331

Cheneil — 2105

Promindo — 1840

Cretaz — 1501
Paquier — 1528

3500m　3000　2500　2000　1500　1000

11 km　10　9　8　7　6　5　4　3　2　1

Section 4.6
COL di NANA

On the opposite side of the stream to the Albergo Panorama at Cheneil is the little chapel of Salus Infirmorum on a prominent spur on the treeline at 2132m. It was built in 1896 and every Easter people come here to be cured of their ailments. Through two tiny windows you can see crutches and walking sticks, abandoned as proof of their cure.

Cheneil is a good place to start for ascents of Monte Roisetta, 3334m, Grand Tournalin, 3379m, and Petit Tournalin, 3207m, as well as Becca Trecare, 3033m, and Becco di Nana, 3010m. All but the first can be tackled from the Col di Nana, but to reach the Grand Tournalin and return to the col, and descend to St. Jacques, would be a very long day.

Details of ascents to Monte Roisetta, Grand Tournalin and Petit Tournalin are given below, while ascents of Becca Trecare and Becco di Nana are described as from the Col di Nana.

Ascents from Cheneil
Monte Roisetta, 3334m

From Cheneil take Path No.23 in the direction of the Salus Infirmorum to Chateau Lezard, 2126m, (only a fancy name for an ordinary chalet) where you can find a small wooden cross in honour of Abate Aimé Gorret (dated 1965). Continue by passing through an enchanting woodland glade at c2300m, beyond which the path climbs a valley and enters the Pasturage de l'Aran, 2585m. The path continues towards the R (in ascent) past Alpe Lezan, 2684m. The path becomes more indistinct as it climbs up below the crest which unites the Becca d'Aran, 2952m, with the Roisetta. From here the three characteristic crags of the Sigari di Bobba are noted on the Roisetta flanks. An easy way on a faint path leads up the crest to the top. 4 hr from Cheneil.

Grand Tournalin, 3379m

From Cheneil take Path No.2/AVVA No.1 SE but just after crossing the second stream, and just before reaching the four-bay cowsheds of Alpe Champsec, 2331m, the paths diverge, Path No.4 to the L being our route for the Grand Tournalin.

Maintain height NE for a little way, then gradually gaining height to the crossing of a third stream at 2470m, 50min. from Cheneil. Then cross a fourth stream twice to arrive at a grassy basin at 2650m in 1hr 15 from Cheneil. Here the path turns E and zig-zags up the SW spur of the Grand Tournalin for a long way - paint splashes so far - then crosses over into the rocky combe at 2910m. (2 hr). At 3070m there is a good "howff" in the boulders then at 3120m you reach the Colletto del Tournalin. (2hr 30min. from Cheneil). This is a narrow rocky crest, grey on one side, red on the other.

Turn N and scramble up the S ridge to the summit, crossing an awkward gap in the crest, which is narrow in parts, then by a final and very narrow crest to the summit, 30min. from the Colletto.

The Grand Tournalin has two tops, a N and a S, the N being some 9m higher. It is an airy traverse between the two. The peak offers a superb panorama of the Breithorn and Liskamm and its ascent is highly recommended.

The mountain was first ascended by Edward Whymper and J. A. Carrel alone on 8 August 1863 - Mont Blanc had been ascended 80 years earlier! At 3370m, just below the summit, are the ruins of a rifugio built by the CAI in 1875 in memory of J. A. Carrel.

The return to the Colletto takes 20min. and from there to Cheneil a leisurely 2hr.

Petit Tournalin, 3207m

The Petit Tournalin merits an ascent in its own right, but it is so close to, and dominated by, the Grand Tournalin that it is often neglected.

Ascend from Cheneil as for the Grand Tournalin but at the Colletto del Tournalin, 3120m, turn R, S, and in 20min. reach the top.

You may also descend the S ridge to Becca Trecare and go on to the Col di Nana.

From Cheneil the path climbs SE - formerly Nos. 2 and 4 but now No. 24A with the AVVA No.1 sign - up to Alpe Champsec, 2331m. Beyond the disused cowsheds, 30min., the path continues as AVVA No.1 and enters a NW-facing combe formed by the Punta Falinere, 2762m, and the Becca Trecare, 3033m, outliers of the Grand Tournalin. The path climbs up to the ridge connecting the two - the Passo del Fontanette (also called the Colle di Croux), 2697m. The Cervino looks magnificent from here and the Grand Paradiso is in the far distance SW.

The path then contours round the head of the Vallone di Chamois and just beyond the outlet of a small pool makes a steeper climb NE to the pass between the Becco di Nana, 3010m, to the S and the Becca Trecare, 3033m, to the N.

[The Col di Nana may be reached more easily from (or via) Chamois, visiting the Sanctuary of Clavite, 2480m, but the Sanctuary is not worth a special visit.

From Cheneil go SW on Path No.107 across the W flank of Punta della Fontana Fredda (also part of the Grande Balconata) to the Colletto di Cheneil, 2277m. (1hr). The path continues towards Chamois, but having passed under the chairlift and reaching Charavellessaz, 2129m, traverse L to Path No. 1A to reach a track at Alpe Glanvin, 2126m. Follow the track, or Path No. 1, winding up to the ridge between Punta dell Fontana Fredda, 2513m, and the Punta Falinere, 2762m. Here, at the end of the track, is the Santuario di Clavalite, 2450m. (1hr from Colletto di Cheneil).

[If staying at Chamois take the chairlift up to 2420m. The Sanctuary is 5min. walk away on an easy ridge to the R. The Chamois chairlift operates summer and winter].

The Sanctuary is dedicated to San Domenico Savio. It is an ugly stone structure with shuttered windows and a feeble attempt at a campanile. Two empty oil drums serve as litter baskets.

From the Sanctuary traverse round the S side on Path No. 1under Punta Falinere and the Passo del Fontanette to the head of the Vallone di Chamois and meet the AVVA No.1 and continue to the Col di Nana. (1hr from the Sanctuary or 3hr on Path No.2 from Corgnolaz to the pass)].

Ascents from the Col di Nana
Becco di Nana, 3010m
This peak to the SSE of the pass is easily reached in less than an hour up the ridge. The mountain is also called the Becco di Falconetta from the numerous hawks which found it cliffs an ideal habitat.
Becca Trecare, 3033m
This peak to the N of the pass is easily reached by going up the L side of the ridge in 30min. The peak is the boundary of the three communes of Valtournanche, Chamois and Ayas. You may continue N along the ridge and go over the Petit Tournalin, 3207m, to the Colletto del Tournalin, 3010m, and even continue along the easy but airy ridge to the Grand Tournalin, 3379m, itself.

There are two signs on the Col di Nana - one saying 2775m, the other 2780m. From the pass both the Becco di Nana and the Becca Trecare can be climbed.

From the Col di Nana the path continues, now Path No.4A, but still AVVA No.1, into the superb combe below the SE face of the Grand Tournalin. It descends to the Alpe Tournalin, 2534m, then follows a jeep road (but cut across the hairpin bends) all the way down the Vallone di Nana. As it enters the trees at Alpe di Nana Inferiore, 2064m, the stream is diverted into the Canale di St. Vincent.

The Canale di St. Vincent is a massive aqueduct (also called the Canale Cortoz) collecting waters from the headwaters of the Evançon at the Vallone di Cortoz at 2100m and carrying it for 25km along the flanks of the Ayas valley to the Font de Napoleon on the Colle di Joux at 1640m, where it is then fed to St. Vincent. It took 40 years to dig at the end of the 14thC by the abbots of Emarese, St. Vincent and Challant St. Anselme, who had obtained in 1393 from the Ibleto of Challant authority to take water from the Ventina Glacier to irrigate their fields.

Just beyond the watercourse the path leaves the road near the Alpe Coones, 1866m, and follows the stream down to Rovinal and the centre of St. Jacques, 1689m. (The road continues into Blanchard, then to St. Jacques).

[Alternatively, from the Col di Nana, Path No.3 goes by the Becco di Nana to Colle di Vascoccia, 2559m, then by Alpe Vascoccia, 2554m, Alpe Mezan, 2016m, across the Canale di St. Vincent and down to Mandran/Mandrioux, then to Magneax, 1704m and finally to Champoluc, 1568m].

SECTION 4.7
COLLE PORTOLA, 2410m

Distance:		**16.5km, Antey St. André to Champoluc**	
		(18.5km via Promiod)	
Height Gain:		**1527m (1661m via Promiod)**	
Height Loss:		**1033m (1167m via Promiod)**	
Grade:		**1**	

Outward		G.B.T.	Return	
		Ant. St. André, 1074m	**6hr 30**	**1hr**
2hr	**2hr**	**Brengon, 1644m**	**5hr 30**	**2hr 45**
2hr 45	**4hr 45**	**Colle Portola, 2410m**	**2hr 45**	**1hr 45**
1hr 45	**6hr 30**	**Antagnod, 1699m**	**1hr**	**1hr**
3hr	**7hr 45**	**St. Jacques, 1689m**		

This is the southernmost pass on the dividing ridge between the Valtournanche and the Valle d'Ayas and one of the easiest. It was crossed by Forbes in 1842 and provides an ascent of Mont Zerbion, 2772m.

Antey St. André, 1074m, is the starting point for this stage, in the Valtournanche mid-way between Paquier and Châtillon. A gradual climb on Path No.11, part of the Grande Balconata, takes you to Brengon, 1644m, the main village of La Magdeleine, or it may be reached in 30min. longer by following the road via Promiod. Alternatively, La Magdeleine may be reached in 1hr from Chamois on a pleasant forestry track, Path No. 107/G.B.

From Brengon go up the road to Artaz c1715m. 100 metres past the Hotel Miravidi take Path No. 4 up between the farmhouses L, soon turning R, then on a sunken path going up L past Nuvole, 1863m. A very steep climb on a good mule track through woods takes you up to c1950m: the track then becomes a path which continues more gradually and you turn the corner of a spur and come out of the woods on the edge of the meadows of Alpe Chancellier di Sopra,

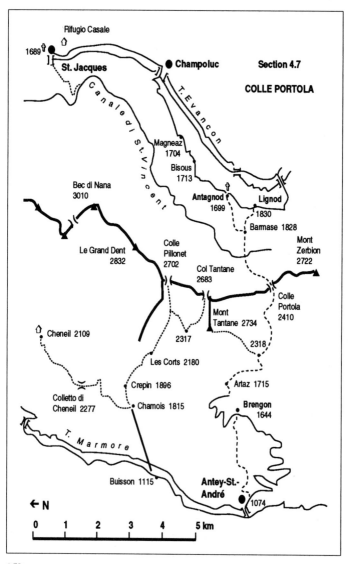

Rifugio Casale
1689
St. Jacques
● Champoluc

Section 4.7

COLLE PORTOLA

T. Evancon

C a n a l e d i S t . V i n c e n t

Magneaz
1704

Bisous
1713

Antagnod
1699
Lignod
1830
Barmase 1828

Bec di Nana
3010

Le Grand Dent
2832

Colle
Pillonet
2702

Col Tantane
2683

Mont
Zerbion
2722

Colle
Portola
2410

Mont
Tantane 2734

2318

Cheneil 2109

2317

Les Corts 2180

Crepin 1896

Artaz 1715

Colletto di
Cheneil 2277

Chamois 1815

Brengon
1644

T. M a r m o r e

Buisson 1115

Antey-St.-
André
1074

← N

0   1   2   3   4   5 km

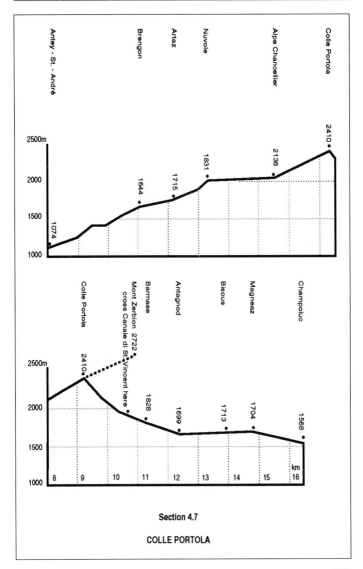

Section 4.7

COLLE PORTOLA

153

2138m, 1hr from Artaz. (Water at spring here). Mont Zerbion, 2772m, with its statue and the Colle Portola are now in full view.

From the farm there is a track contouring round the valley which meets another track coming up from the Promiod valley to La Nuova, 2193m. A track is seen ahead which appears to be a continuation and which appears to go to the Colle Portola, but this is not so. That track was used when the WT reflector station was built on a col some 500 metres N of the Colle Portola. Our pass requires a traverse round to the R. Both cols are crossed by power lines, but the southernmost is the one we want.

The view from the Colle Portola is extensive, from Becca Trecaré and the Grand Tournalin on the L and the whole of the Breithorn - Liskamm - Monte Rosa ridge in the centre and the Testa Grigia opposite with Champoluc below.

The Colle Portola is a notch in a ridge of shaly rock that steeply overhangs the Valle d'Ayas. The first 100m or so of descent on Path No. 2/105 is somewhat awkward though rapid, then it is easier over rocks, scree and grass. It follows the edge of the treeline and a funnel of open ground and meets the Canale di St. Vincent, c1950m, then descends through the trees to the village of Antagnod, 1699m. Here follow the road southwards through Lignod, 1630m, to descend to the main valley road or, preferably, follow the road northwards through Bisous and Magneaz, 1704m, descending gradually to Champoluc, 1568m.

[Alternatively, from the meeting with the Canale di St. Vincent, follow the aqueduct northwards on Path No. 5 via rustic bridges and seats to St. Jacques. Allow 3hr for this delightful walk, with views of the Monte Rosa massif in view ahead through clearings between the trees or across open meadows.

Close to Alpe di Varda, 2052m, near St. Jacques, a rockfall has destroyed the canal and engineers have constructed a new underground pipeline that reaches the canal at this point. Therefore, 5min. after the pipeline feeder, leave the aqueduct and descend awkwardly to Alpe di Varda, seen below through the trees. Go to the northern end of its meadows and find a faint path - little used and somewhat

154

overgrown - that descends through the larch woods to cross the Torrente di Nana by a new bridge, then across meadows to Rovinal, 1711m, and so to St. Jacques].

The Colle Portola, 2410m

The Colle Portola was crossed by Forbes in 1842 on his (shorter) Tour of Monte Rosa from Zermatt.

Forbes and his party left Zermatt at 4.30am, crossed the Théodule and arrived at Breuil at 2pm, having stayed an hour with the two Spanish *'douaniers'* at the customs post on the frontier. They walked down the road from Breuil *"leisurely, having the afternoon before us"* and slept at Valtournanche.

They left the village at 7.30am next morning, on 27 August 1842, and *"descended the valley a little way further; we then took a footpath on the left, and soon found ourselves in a wood, which covers the precipices of that part of the valley... Our footpath, which was a short cut,* (today's Path No.26) *soon split into numberless tracks and as we gradually got among the rocks, we were glad that we were not left to waste time by discovering a way for ourselves. As we ascended gradually higher and higher, and all the while, as we walked parallel to the course of the valley, the torrent was working itself deeper and deeper, so that from each fresh crag we found a greater interval between us and it, until at last, turning a rock, we stood above a precipice at least 2000 feet high to which here and there a clinging pine seemed to give more steepness, by offering a scale for measuring the abyss. This point gained, we rejoiced in the beauty of the morning, and of the herbage spangled with drops from the early mists; and as we turned round we saw behind us the Mont Cervin rising in unclouded splendour. We then passed from rock and wood to an open Alpine pasturage* (L'Avore, 1927m) *which seemed cut off by these precipices from the world beneath, and here was the house of (our guide), a little village, appropriately named Chamois, one and a half hour distant from Val Tournanche.*

"From thence, a gentle though pretty long ascent took us to the Col de Portola, composed of limestone, and very precipitous on the eastern side, where it immediately overlooks the village of Ayas. ... The descent presented no difficulty, and from Ayas two hours' pleasant walk took us to Brusson. ... We arrived at Brusson soon after three ..."

Ascents from Colle Portola
Mont Zerbion, 2772m

Mont Zerbion is easily accessible in 45min. from the pass up the ridge to the S. A path winds up below the ridge on its W side, runs round a rib, gains a level area before the final scree slopes take you to the top. A large statue of the Madonna stands on the highest point. Erected in 1932 it was restored in 1968 "In lega leggera". The summit commands an extensive view, with Mont Emilius, 3559m, above Aosta and the Gran Paradiso beyond.

Mont Tantané, 2734m

Go N from the pass on Path No. 5 for 2hr. Easy, though not to be recommended in a strong W wind! Go over Point 2475m to the next col, where the WT reflector station is sited, then avoid Point 2540m by going on its W side. Turn W off the main ridge to the summit, topped by a large cross.

SECTION 5
VALLE d'AYAS to VAL di GRESSONEY

The Valle d'Ayas is a very beautiful valley and is relatively untouched by the scars of ski development, although it is the western of the three valleys that form the Monterosa Ski area based in Champoluc.

The valley enters the main valley of the Dora Baltea at Verres, 432m, and the road goes past the two villages of Challant Saint Victor and Challant Saint Anselme, which gave their name to the powerful medieval feudal dynasty, the lords of the entire Valle d'Ayas. It is said that the inhabitants of certain villages in the glen held their own lands by the quaint tenure of covering with earth the glacier on the Becca Torche, 3016m, to the SE of the settlements, so that the complexion of the ladies of the house of Challant might not suffer from the glare during their summer sojourn at the castle of Graines. The fine ruins of the Castle of Graines is just above the valley floor between Challant and Brusson.

Brusson lies 16km up the valley at about mid-way point, beneath the Corno Bussola, 3024m. It is situated on the route from Aosta to Gressoney, a route via St. Vincent and the Colle di Joux, 1640m, now a highway with a bus route, continuing as a minor road on the east side over the Colle de Ranzola, 2170m, to Gressoney St. Jean.

In medieval times the village belonged to the men of Graines, who in their turn depended upon the Abbey of St. Maurice of Agaune. The parish church was built in the 12thC and rebuilt in the second half of the 19thC. It has a fine 15thC campanile.

A further 10km up the valley is the scattered commune of Ayas, which gives its name to the valley. Flanked by the hills in a broad curve of the valley it has a good view of the mass of Monte Rosa and its neighbouring 4000m peaks and their hanging glaciers. The parish church at Antagnod dates from the 15thC and has a valuable artistic work in its Baroque altar. There is also the House of Challant at Antagnod. The bell in the neighbouring church at Lignod is 15thC.

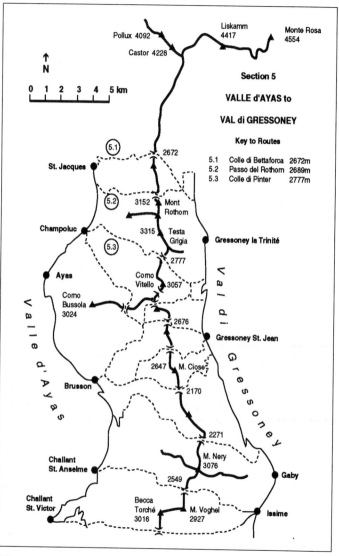

Pollux 4092

Castor 4228

Liskamm 4417

Monte Rosa 4554

↑
N

0 1 2 3 4 5 km

5.1

St. Jacques

2672

5.2

3152 Mont Rothorn

3315 Testa Grigia

Champoluc

5.3

Gressoney la Trinité

2777

Ayas

Corno Vitello 3057

Corno Bussola 3024

2676

Gressoney St. Jean

Brusson

2647 M. Ciose

2170

2271

M. Nery 3076

Challant St. Anselme

2549

Gaby

Challant St. Victor

Becca Torché 3016

M. Voghel 2927

Issime

Section 5

VALLE d'AYAS to

VAL di GRESSONEY

Key to Routes

5.1 Colle di Bettaforca 2672m
5.2 Passo del Rothorn 2689m
5.3 Colle di Pinter 2777m

Valle d'Ayas

Val di Gressoney

Ayas and neighbouring Champoluc are on the routes that pass over the Colle Tantané and Colle Portola to the W and the Colle di Pinter and Passo del Rothorn to the E.

Champoluc is a busy little place and on its northern outskirts is the *télécabine* station for Crest. (Small supermarket nearby). Five minutes up the road is the small Albergo Rhododendro and 10min. further is the Albergo Monte Cervino. Fifteen minutes further up the valley is Frachey, 1614m.

[There is a pleasant walk on a track on the R bank of the Evançon between Champoluc and Frachey. From the car park on the outskirts of Champoluc a bridge crosses the river, and you cross over to reach the road again at Frachey].

Just above Frachey is the roadhead village of St. Jacques, 1689m, or San Giacomo d'Ayas, at the confluence of torrents from the Avantina glacier and the Vera glacier, the united stream being called the Torrente Evançon.

St. Jacques is a 'Walser' village: the dialect of the inhabitants in this upper part of the valley is rather different from the usual patois of the tributary glens of the Dora Baltea valley, and may represent an early form of Romansch.

The Church of St. Jacques probably dates from 1500 although it was rebuilt in 1872. Underneath the Gothic arch in the altar are important frescoes of Calvary. Adjoining the church is 'la Rettoria' founded in 1712, with wooden balconies, and on its wall, behind the church, is a tablet to Abate Gorret (b. 25 October 1836, d. 4 November 1907)who lived here for 21 years whilst rector of St. Jacques. In the street adjoining is a good example of a 'rascard' house - buildings typical of Walser architecture.

The main square of St. Jacques is the Place de la Grote, principally used today as a car park. A grotto above the water supply in the square has a chapel founded by Abbot Jean Baptiste Lemonnier (b.1839), Rector of St. Jacques from 1905 until his death in 1925, aged 86.

The Place de la Grote has its souvenir shops and a small shop having a good stock of supplies - cheese, ham, torta, fruit - and bakes its own bread fresh in the mornings. There was until recently a lovely old bar opposite the parish church, but sadly it is now closed. The bus terminus is just below the village.

Of all the main ranges that run S of the frontier watershed of the Pennine Alps those that flank the Valle di Gressoney are the two that run more consistently to the vertical of the axis than the remainder. The range of the W side separating the valley from the Valle d'Ayas to the W runs consistently N-S for more than 33km.

This range starts at Zwillinge/I Gemelli/The Twins - Castor and Pollux - and has more summits higher than 3000m than the range just crossed to the W. In contrast, the passes over this range are generally lower than those over the range to the W.

Apart from the high alpine passes over and close to the frontier there are eleven other passes over the range to choose from. The northernmost is the Passo di Bettolina, 2905m, N of the Colle di Bettaforca, a walker's pass but unsuitable for our purposes. It would be used as an alternative to the Colle di Bettaforca only if ascending (or descending) the ridge running N to the Rifugio Quintino Sella. There are seven passes S of the Colle di Pinter, but these are too far S to be of any practical use for our circuit. From N to S these are: Passo di Valfreda, 2804m; Passo di Valnera, 2676m; Passo della Bochetta, 2562m; Colle della Ranzola, 2170m; Passo di Frudiera, 2271m; Colle di Chasten, 2549m; and Colle Dondeuil, 2338m.

The passes described in this guide, from N to S are:

Section	Pass	Height	Grade	Quality
5.1	Colle di Bettaforca	2672m	1	
5.2	Passo del Rothorn	2689m	3	***
5.3	Colle di Pinter	2777m	3	***

All of these routes are shown on the Studio FMB map, LS Map 294 Gressoney, the IGC Sheet 5 Cervino/Matterhorn & Monte Rosa, and Kompass Sheet 876 Breuil/Cervinia-Zermatt.

Scarpia, 1726m, in the Valle d'Otro (Section 6)

Pianmissura, 1854m, Valle d'Otro
Follu, 1664m, Valle d'Otro

SECTION 5.1
COLLE di BETTAFORCA, 2672m

Distance:	**12km, St. Jacques to Gressoney-la-Trinité**
Height Gain:	**1033m**
Height Loss:	**1098m**
Grade:	**1**

Outward		G.B.T.	Return	
		St. Jacques, 1689m	6hr 30	45min.
1hr	1hr	Resy, 2072m	5hr 45	35min.
45min.	1hr 45	Alpe Forca, 2331m	5hr 10	40min.
45min.	2hr 30	Colle di Bettaforca, 2672m	4hr 30	2hr
45min.	3hr 15	Alpe Sitten, 2218m	2hr 30	1hr 30
55min.	4hr 10	Staffal, 1850m	1hr	1hr
50min.	5hr	Gressoney-la-Trinité, 1624m		

There is a direct ascent to the Colle from St. Jacques via the Forca glen. Both the ascent and descent are largely on ski roads and pistes and disfigured by ski developments, and as a consequence the route is easy but uninteresting.

Leave the village square of St. Jacques, 1689m, on the N side, pass the church then turn R past houses on the road, soon becoming a path (No.52). There is a stiff climb up through the woods to Rascard, 1887m, and to the treeline at Alpe Resy, where there are two private huts - Rifugio Ferraro and Rifugio delle Guide Frachey - converted from old *'rascards'*. That of Ferraro is dated 1586. Rifugio Ferraro is marked 2066m, but both map and altimeter read 2072m.

[Alternatively, Path No.5 coming in from the N via Fiéry, or Path No.6 from the S, coming off the road at Ciarcerio, 1975m, above the CAI Rifugio Casale Monferrato.]

These two private rifugi have access by the jeep road/piste coming over the Colle di Bettaforca from Staffal. Unfortunately this is our

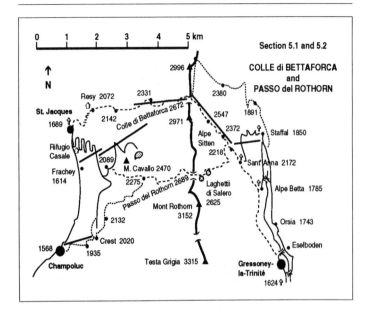

route too: an unpleasant climb up shale and stones to the windswept pass. There is no shelter, except in the functional chairlift station on the ridge to the north.

Our route descends another jeep road/piste southeasterly, accompanied by the chairlift coming up from Staffal, 1850m. The monotony is relieved with a view of the Corno Bianco, 3320m ahead and the view leftwards to the Col d'Olen, 2881m. From the vantage point of the bar/restaurant at Alpe Sitten, 2218m, you can plot the route for the next stage of the journey. From Alpe Sitten you can either descend the chairlift down to Staffal, 1850m, for accommodation or for buses to Gressoney or gondolas to Gabiet, or continue on Path No.9 to the chapel of Sant' Anna, 2172m, where there is a good view of Gressoney-la-Trinité. At he chapel turn R to cross the stream in the valley and continue down Path No.9 to reach the main valley of the Torrente Lys and into Gressoney-la-Trinité.

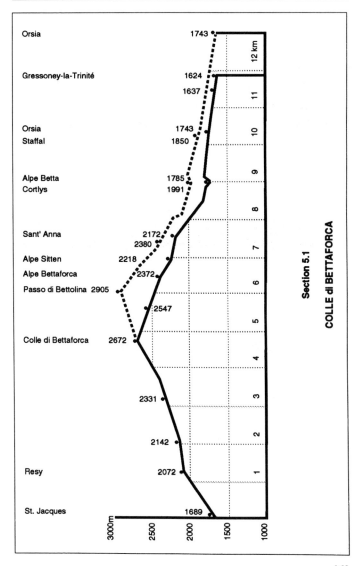

Section 5.1

COLLE di BETTAFORCA

Orsia — 1743

Gressoney-la-Trinité — 1624
1637

Orsia — 1743
Staffal — 1850

Alpe Betta — 1785
Cortlys — 1991

Sant' Anna — 2172
2380

Alpe Sitten — 2218

Alpe Bettaforca — 2372

Passo di Bettolina — 2905

2547

Colle di Bettaforca — 2672

2331

2142

Resy — 2072

St. Jacques — 1689

Rascards at Resy, 2072m.

Having come into the Valle d'Ayas one September day in 1855 from St. Vincent by crossing the Colle di Joux above Brusson and travelled up the valley, the Rev. King and his party stayed the night in the lonely chalets of Soussun, 1945m, directly above the village of Frachey, not far from St. Jacques.

"But we had to sup in public. Our arrival had created an immense sensation ... and one by one the whole of the settlement, master, mistress, domestic, and herdsmen - of whom there were a considerable number - with all their children, came in and seated themselves in a grave wondering now all round the sides of the room, whispering comments at our movements. Their curiosity was especially excited as we occasionally brought little things out of the saddle-bags, such as spoons, pepper and salt, candles, silver mug, thermometer, maps, etc., which were all eagerly discussed in turn."

The following morning the crowd returned and watched King making observations on the temperature of boiling water: *"Like our meals, my proceedings were watched by all the unemployed people of this singular little colony, who, as they sat round the fire of wood embers in the shed which served as a kitchen, intently looking on, seemed utterly at a loss what I was going to make out of a boiled thermometer, an instrument they had never seen or heard of before, and gravely asked me if it were some device of magic. When, however, I explained the instrument to them, and showed the proportionate rise and fall of mercury with hot and cold water, the warm hand and the cold air outside, they were greatly delighted and astonished."*

When they left they traversed round the hillside, on a good path through the woods, into the Vallone della Forca and soon reached the Colle di Bettaforca but *"by the time we reached the summit the clouds had permanently settled down for the day. ... The limited view was wide and dreary enough."* They stayed no longer on the pass than was necessary and descended in thick fog all the way down into the Val de Lys, through La Trinité to St. Jean, hoping to stay in the house that Forbes had used several years earlier.

They noted that the passing greeting of all the peasants they met were in German, the Teutonic accents being strange after the Piedmontese patois they had been so long accustomed to. They noted too that the distinct costume of a dark blue cloth jacket over a scarlet woollen shirt, and a bright-coloured handkerchief tied behind the head, was universal among the women.

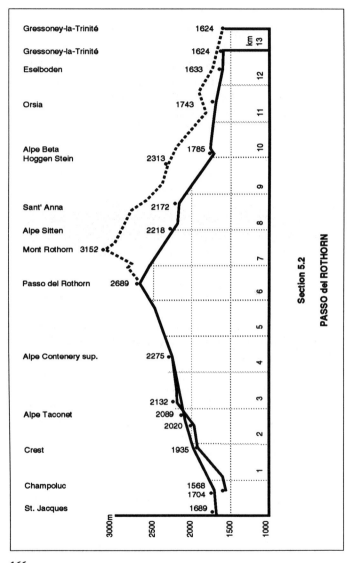

Section 5.2

PASSO del ROTHORN

Location	Elevation
Gressoney-la-Trinité	1624
Gressoney-la-Trinité	1624
Eselboden	1633
Orsia	1743
Alpe Beta	1785
Hoggen Stein	2313
Sant' Anna	2172
Alpe Sitten	2218
Mont Rothorn	3152
Passo del Rothorn	2689
Alpe Contenery sup.	2275
	2132
Alpe Taconet	2089
	2020
Crest	1935
Champoluc	1568
	1704
St. Jacques	1689

SECTION 5.2
PASSO del ROTHORN, 2698m

Distance:	12.9km, St Jacques to Gressoney-la-Trinité
	(12.2km, Champoluc to Gressoney-Trinité)
Height Gain:	1351m (1472m from Champoluc)
Height Loss:	1166m
Grade:	3***

Outward		G.B.T.	Return	
		St. Jacques, 1689m	6hr 30	1hr
2hr	2hr	Alpe Contenery, 2248m	5hr 30	1hr
1hr	3hr	Passo del Rothorn, 2689m	4hr 30	2hr
45min.	3hr 45	Sitten, 2218m	2hr 30	1hr 30
1hr	4hr 45	Staffal, 1825m	1hr	1hr
45min.	5hr 30	Gressoney-la-Trinité, 1624m		

This route avoids the scars of the Colle di Bettaforca and enables an ascent to be made of the Rothorn, 3152m. It is a beautiful route.

From St. Jacques go S down the main valley road and then L up the minor road past the CAI Rifugio Casale Monferrato. Here turn L on a forestry road, waymarked, zig-zagging E uphill to the old chalets of Alpe Ciarcierio Inferiore, 1975m, as if on the AVVA No.1. Here a double chairlift comes up from Frachey and a quad chair goes up towards the Bettaforca (called Alpe Mandria). (This lift enables skiers to use another lift to the Colle di Bettaforca and so ski down either side of that pass).

The forestry road rises beyond the chairlift interchange and then at a Y fork you turn up L on track No. 10 to Alpe Taconet, 2089m. Here turn R on a path through the woods, climbing over the lip of a coomb into the bowl of Alpe Contenery, 2248m, and underneath a chairlift that goes to Lago Ciarcierio, 2376m, underneath the peaklet of Mont Cavallo, 2470m.

Continue into the Contenery glen and at the upper chalets of the same name, 2275m, cross a ski road coming from Crest and going to Lago Ciarcierio. Go up the grassy piste a short way, with the stream on your L, and after a short distance quit the piste and follow the marked path into the upper glen. When this narrows the path ascends by zig-zags the edge of the glen, then at c2460m reaches a delightful upper corrie and the pass is seen ahead. The path tends to keep to the R of the stream, then when the glacial debris is reached crosses to the L over large stone blocks, trying to find grass where it can, to reach the pass, 2698m.

Ascent of Monte Rothorn, 3152m

Monte Rothorn, to the S of the Passo del Rothorn, was first ascended, from the pass, by H. B. de Saussure on 10 August 1789. The summit may be reached without difficulty in 1hr, although it is a very rocky route amongst loose blocks all of the way. Go up to the Passo Superiore del Rothorn and turn L. The ascent is an extra 520m height gain and loss and an extra 1km in distance.

The summit is infrequently visited, in spite of the superb panorama from the top. To the N rise the snowy domes of the frontier ridge through the Plan Rosa, Breithorn, Pollux, Castor and Liskamm; to the NW is the Grand Tournalin; to the SE Corno Bianco, while due S, very close, is the dominating Testa Grigia.

If you have ascended Monte Rothorn, a direct but steep descent goes SE across the flanks of the Monte Rothorn - Testa Grigia slopes to the Hoggen Stein, 2313m, (also called Hockenestei) on Path No.10 to Cappella dei Morti, 1624m, the cemetery at Gressoney-la-Trinité, in 3hr.

The eastward view from the Passo del Rothorn, 2698m.

The Passo del Rothorn is wide and rocky, with shelter among the rocks immediately below the E side.

The view ahead is of the Stolemberg, 3202m, with the Col d'Olen, 2881m, to the L. (usually with snow patches). To the R comes the pointed Corno Rosso, 3023m, and the Colle di Zube, 2874m, rising to Punta di Straling, 3115m, and the Corno Grosso, 3042m. The Corno Bianco, 3280m, just peeps out behind the flank of Monte Rothorn. The ski developments at Gabiet occupy the lower ground, with the Vallone di Mos just over the lip of the corrie containing the two Laghetti del Salero. The backward view is of Mont Emilius, 3559m, to the L with the Colle Portola just out of sight (although it has been in view in the ascent). Then comes Mont Tantané, 2734m. Further to the R, directly behind you, the Col di Nana, 2780m, is the most obvious pass, with the Grand Tournalin group to the R.

From the Passo del Rothorn Path No.8A descends in 5min. to two small lakes, the Laghetti del Salero, 2625m. Keep to the L of their outlets (more shelter amongst rocks on L at outlet of lower lake) and follow the stream, crossing and recrossing, reaching another delightful basin, then when the path turns away from the stream it descends steeply and traverses, sometimes precariously, on a grass and earth path to about the 2500m contour, then turns away N across the bowl of the valley to Sitten, 2218m, the change-over point of the chairlifts from where you can descend to Staffal, 1850m. The bar/restaurant at Sitten is confusingly called Henniger Hutte. (Note the various spellings of Sitte/Sitten; Staffal/Stafal/Staval and Gaval/Ciaval/Tschavel, reflecting the Romansch origins).

If you want to walk down the ski road to Staffal allow another hour from Sitten. There is expensive accommodation at Staffal, but if you need accommodation at Gabiet go up Path No.7A/AVVA No. 3 or alternatively take the new gondola.

There is a greater choice of accommodation at Gressoney-la-Trinité and Esselboden. Esselboden has some modern hotels and is clustered around the chairlift to Punta Jolanda but the main settlement at Gressoney-la-Trinité, 1624m, just across the river, has more traditional accommodation to offer.

SECTION 5.3
COLLE di PINTER, 2777m

Distance:	11.8km Champoluc to Gressoney-la-Trinité	
Height Gain:	1209m	
Height Loss:	1131m	
Grade:	3***	

Outward		G.B.T.	Return	
		Champoluc, 1568m	7hr 15	30min.
2hr	2hr	Crest, 1935m	6hr 45	30min.
1hr	3hr	Cuneaz, 2032m	6hr 45	1hr 30
1hr 30	4hr 30	Colle di Pinter, 2777m	4hr 45	4hr 30
2hr	6hr 30	Chemonal, 1407m	15min.	15min.
15min.	6hr 45	Gressoney-la-Trinité, 1646m		

The Colle di Pinter (or Pinterjoch or Col de Cuneaz) is directly ascended from Champoluc. It is the most practical southernmost pass between the Ayas and Lys valleys for a Tour of Monte Rosa. It is also the last stage of the route of the AVVA No.1.

The traverse of the pass also enables an ascent to be made of the Testa Grigia, 3315m, (not to be confused with the Testa Grigia on the Plateau Rosa) an ascent of which should not be omitted if the walker is favoured with fine weather.

Leave the centre of Champoluc, 1568m, on Path No.11A, climbing steeply up through woods above the Torrent di Cuneaz to reach the hotels and ski lift developments among the chalets at Crest, 1935m, just above the treeline.

[Alternatively, take the Champoluc-Crest *télécabine*. The stage is 15min. Operates from 14 July - 2 September, daily 08.00-12.50 and 14.00-17.50].

[Alternatively, from St. Jacques or Resy, follow a jeep track contouring round the hillside through the woods. This is the AVVA

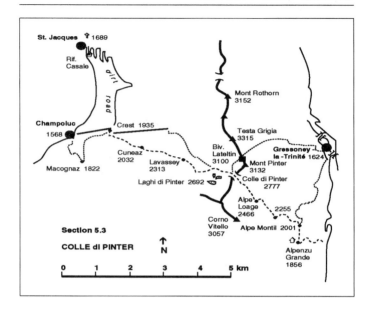

Section 5.3

COLLE di PINTER

Looking south from Mont Pinter, 3132m.

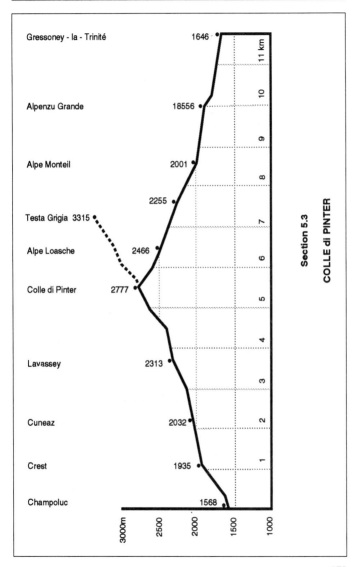

Section 5.3

COLLE di PINTER

No.1. (1hr from Resy or 1hr 50min. from St. Jacques. Same time for return)].

At Crest there is accommodation at the Albergo Edelweiss beside the telecabine top station from Champoluc, while a little higher up the hillside is the Albergo Creforné. Up the valley at Ostafa is a bar.

At Crest and beyond, the paths on the ground have been re-numbered since maps were printed. Paths from Crest to the Colle di Pinter are Nos.11A, 13C and 12. (No.6 goes to the Testa Grigia). Path 11A is steeper in parts than No.12, especially at the headwall of the valley. No.11A is also the AVVA No.1 and one sees several parties of teenagers on it overloaded with large rucksacks.

From Crest the greater part of the ascent on Path No.11A is easy enough, passing Cuneaz, 2032m, and Lavassey, 2313m, and at intervals fine views of the Matterhorn are seen. At about 2400m the way becomes steep and difficult where the path lies along the W (L) bank of a waterfall coming down the valley headwall, but at 2690m the gradient eases and Path No.12 comes in on the L. (The stream comes out of a side valley on the R where there are the three Laghi di Pinter, 2692m, a popular spot for visitors from Champoluc). In 5 min. more the path reaches the crest of the pass. There is a cairn but no shelter, and there is a trickle of water just below the pass on the W side for a refreshing drink.

[Alternatively, the Crest-Ostafa chairlift is a 15min. stage to the top station, c2430m. Operating period same dates as the telecabine, but hours 08.30-12.30 and 14.15-17.15.

From the top station of the chairlift at Ostafa, Path No.12 (not marked on some maps) traverses at a higher level across the slopes, above the Lavassey cliffs, steep in parts, and meets the main Path No.11A beside the stream at 2690m in an hour. The pass is 5min. away].

Rascards at Cuneaz, 2032m.

Ascent of Testa Grigia, 3315m

From the Colle di Pinter there is an easy scramble up to the Testa Grigia, which should not be missed if the weather is clear and if you have the time: 2hr 30min. for the return trip.

The Testa Grigia (or Grauhaupt) is one of the most frequented peaks on the ridge between the Valle d'Ayas and the Val de Lys on account of its celebrated panorama, perhaps the finest on the southern side of the Monte Rosa chain as it overtops all the nearer summits. On clear days you can see all the peaks from the Monte Viso to the Ortler.

The peak was first ascended by the S ridge in 1858 and the Abate Gorret made the first ascent up the N ridge in 1873.

The climb from the Colle di Pinter is rough, over and amidst large loose blocks on the SW face of Monte Pinter as far as Mont Pinter's connecting ridge. 1hr from the pass (at 360m/hr). The last few metres to this connecting ridge are very easy.

[By turning R at the ridge along its crest you come to the top of Monte Pinter, 3132m. Just beyond and below the top is the Bivacco Ulrich Lateltin, 3124m, at the front of which and on the edge of a cliff is a cross, which can be seen from the Colle. The Bivacco is a large domed tin hut, built in 1984. It has two tiers of sleeping platforms with mattresses and blankets for 16, but it will sleep more. There is no water nearby].

The Testa Grigia is almost 1km to the NW along the connecting ridge and is only a 30min. scramble from the bivouac hut (slightly less from the point of arrival on the connecting ridge). After passing beneath two crumbling shale towers on a poor path a chain provides a pull up of 2m on to the SE ridge, followed by a traverse on a narrow exposed ledge on the E side overlooking Gressoney, then finally a pull up another chain on the side wall of a gully to the top. The ledge is a delicate spot, but a fine situation to be in, so close to the summit.

The Mont Cenis bellflower, *Campanula cenisia,* King of the Alps, *Eritrichium nanum,* the Alpine toadflax, *Linaria alpina,* and the Alpine sedge, *Carex curvula,* and a few other flowering plants have been found close to the summit.

[From the connecting ridge between the two peaks of Pinter and Testa Grigia Path No.10C descends to Gressoney-la-Trinité, but it is steeper and less well used than the Colle di Pinter route. The Bivacco Virgilio Cozzi which stood at 2750m below the E face of the Testa Grigia, on this path, and still shown on some maps, has been demolished].

The descent from the Colle di Pinter towards the Val de Lys is easy, and practicable for mules. The path, now No.6, follows above the R bank of the Rio Montil in a SE direction across Alpe Loage. (30min. to Alpe Loage Supperiore, 2466m. Water. Then Alpe Loage, 2365m, and Alpe Loage Inferiore, 2255m). The last part of the descent, below Montil, 2001m, is steep. The path zig-zags down through woods beside a waterfall and passes through Alpenzu Grande, 1779m, a Walser settlement on the Grande Sentiero Walser or Walserweg, a route running down the W side of the Valle di Gressoney connecting Walser settlements. There is refugio accommodation here. The path, now Nos. 5A and 6, drops steeply through the woods to the main road in the valley at Chemonal, 1407m, about mid-way between Gressoney-St.-Jean and Gressoney-la-Trinité.

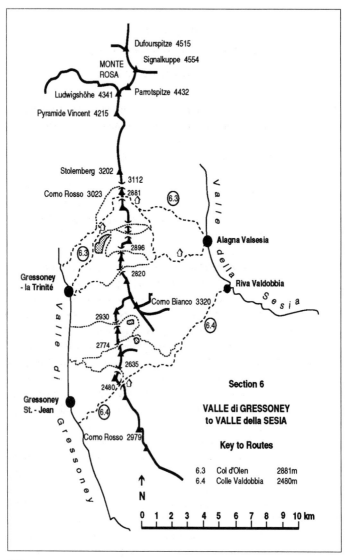

Dufourspitze 4515

Signalkuppe 4554

MONTE ROSA

Ludwigshöhe 4341   Parrotspitze 4432

Pyramide Vincent 4215

Stolemberg 3202   3112
                         2881
Como Rosso 3023   6.3

6.3

Gressoney - la Trinité   2896

                         2820

                    Como Bianco 3320   Alagna Valsesia

                                              Riva Valdobbia

                                              Sesia

2930   6.4

2774

2635

Gressoney St. - Jean   2480

6.4   **Section 6**

Como Rosso 2979   **VALLE di GRESSONEY**
                         to VALLE della SESIA

                         Key to Routes

Valle di Gressoney

↑
N

                    6.3   Col d'Olen   2881m
                    6.4   Colle Valdobbia   2480m

0 1 2 3 4 5 6 7 8 9 10 km

SECTION 6
VALLE di GRESSONEY
to VALLE della SESIA

The Valle di Gressoney is the name given to the valley carrying the Torrente Lys, the Val de Lys being its other name. It is remarkably straight in its upper reaches and certainly not as sinuous in its lower reaches as the adjoining Valle d'Ayas to the W, whereas the adjoining Valle della Sesia to the E is sinuous throughout.

The valley is sometimes called the "Trilingual valley of Monte Rosa". The principal tongue is Walser, a German dialect resembling that found in the Upper Valais of Switzerland, but spoken exclusively in the upper valley basin. [It is known that long before 1218 this basin was a fief of the Bishops of Sion, who, probably before that date, brought in Valaisan colonists and encouraged the immigration of Walser shepherds over the St. Théodule, to guarantee his control of the area against the Challant family - those Counts of Savoy who built their castles in the Val d'Aosta. The Valaisan settlement here has historically nothing to do with that of Macugnaga, which is known to have taken place from the Saas valley some 30-80 years later].

The second language is the Valaisan patois closely resembling the German tongue, while the third, in a minority, is Italian. In all of these valleys S of Monte Rosa the ethnic groups have preserved their dialect and customs, local traditions and costumes and traditional style of buildings.

The valley takes its name from the two principal settlements of Gressoney-St.-Jean and Gressoney-la-Trinité, most typically Alpine-looking villages with traditional stone and wood chalet-style buildings. St. Jean is the larger of the two, and is situated at 1385m, some 26km up the valley from its mouth at Pont St. Martin. La Trinité is 6km further up the valley, at 1685m, about a quarter the size of St. Jean. The situation of these villages, amidst meadows and fruit trees, and yet in full view of the eternal snows, is very beautiful. There are numerous old houses in the valley, with the ground floor in stone and the upper part in wood, with balconies in wood round three sides, in the manner of the Walser immigrants from Germany. They are known as *'rascards'*.

St. Jean, and to a lesser extent La Trinité, have grown with hotels and holiday chalets to cater for the growth in ski developments in the area: Gressoney is the centre of the 'Monte Rosa Ski' region. Nevertheless there are still some attractive corners: the parish church of La Trinité dates from the 16thC and was built on the site of an earlier church. One tablet on the church records the memory of Johann Nicholas Vincent of Gressoney, who climbed the Pyramide Vincent, 4215m, on 5August 1819. In the attached churchyard are massive tombs to the local families of Fritz Thedy and Busca. The massive Hotel Busca Thedy has seen better days and appears to be in mothballs. The 18thC church of St. Jean has a portico dated 1630.

About 4.5km above St. Jean and 1.5km below La Trinité is Noversch, where a narrow pack horse bridge dated 1560 spans a deep ravine carrying the Lys torrent. Noversch was the home of Joseph Zumstein (1783-1861), one of the early explorers of the upper regions of the Monte Rosa group. [In 1820 Zumstein ascended the third highest peak of the Monte Rosa, the Zumsteinspitze, 4563m. No-one climbed higher on Monte Rosa than Zumstein until 1855 when the Dufourspitze, 4634m, the highest summit, was attained. The second highest peak, Nordend, 4609m, was not reached until 1861].

In a very fine position at a sudden drop in the floor of the valley, 0.5km above Noversch, is the splendid Hotel Miravelle, used by visiting climbers and admirers of Zumstein.

Further up the valley, at the roadhead, some 3km above La Trinité, is Stavel. This former hunting lodge belonged to the Baron de Pecoz, whose family, of Gressoney origin, made its fortune in Germany and was ennobled by the King of Bavaria. The Baron was a great chamois hunter and in his house is deposited his collection of stuffed animals and birds, killed by himself, which deserves a visit. At Stavel Baron de Pecoz once entertained the sons of the King of Sardinia and his villa was used several times as a summer residence of Margherita, the Queen of Italy. "Stavel" is the local patois form of Staffel.

The ridge running S from the Pyramide Vincent, dividing the Val de Lys from the Valle della Sesia, lies parallel to its counterpart on the W side of the valley for a distance of about 14km (as far as the Colle Valdobbia, almost due E of Gressoney-St.-Jean) but then it follows a more sinuous course for a greater distance until it runs out in the foothills towards Milan.

For our purposes of making a circuit of Monte Rosa we need only consider two of the ten passes across the ridge in its upper half. Seven of these ten routes cross unfrequented passes that connect Gressoney-la-Trinité with Alagna Valsesia. Two pass to the N of the Punta di Straling, 3115m - the Colle di Zube, 2874m, and the Passo di Civera, 2896m - and two pass to the S - the Passo della Coppa, 2916m, and the Passo dell'Uomo Storto, 2820m, and approach Alagna direct by the Val d'Otro. Three other routes - the Passo di Rissuolo, 2930m, the Passo dell'Alpetto, 2774m, and the Passo di Valdobbiola, 2635m - cross the ridge to the S of the Corno Bianco, 3320m, before dropping down into the Val Vogna. All seven are adventurous routes, rough and steep, suitable only for mountaineers, and outside the scope of this guide. An eighth pass, the Colle delle Pisse, 3112m, to the N of the Col d'Olen, is likely to be used by those gaining access to the high mountain huts, and is therefore outside the scope of this guide. Only the following two routes may be considered to be walkers' passes, at the N and S of this half of the range, namely:

Section	Pass	Height	Grade	Quality
6.3	Col d'Olen	2881m	3	***
6.4	Colle Valdobbia	2480m	3	**

Both routes are shown on LS Map 294 Gressoney, IGC Sheet 5 Cervino/Matterhorn & Monte Rosa, Kompass Sheet 88 Monte Rosa and on the Studio FMB Map.

SECTION 6.1
The ASCENT of MONTE ROSA

Just as Breuil was the jumping-off point for ascents of the Cervino, so was Gressoney the base for ascents of the Monte Rosa.

The peasants in the valleys below Monte Rosa believed that a 'happy valley' was hidden away among the glaciers of the range of mountains at the head of the Gressoney valley, a valley in which flowers blossomed in winter and in which cattle were never driven down from their pastures by the snow.

It was a rumour that the men of Alagna in Val Sesia were determined to find this fabled valley that incited the men of Gressoney to anticipate them. One Sunday morning - 22 August 1778 - a party of seven men, led by Giovanni Nicola Vincent, set out on the adventurous quest to discover the 'happy valley.'

The party gained a rocky tooth just W of the lowest depression in the ridge - i.e. just W of the Lysjoch - on the watershed. This was named by them the "Discovery Rock" - Roccia della Scoperta/ Entdeckungfels - as from it they looked down on the 'lost valley', filled in its higher part by the ice of the Gornergletscher and girdled by a long line of savage peaks from the Mischabelhorn to the Dent Blanche.

"It was 12 o'clock. Hardly had we got to the summit of the rock than we saw a grand, an amazing spectacle. We sat down to contemplate at our leisure the lost valley, which seemed to us to be entirely covered with glaciers. We examined it carefully, but could not satisfy ourselves that it was the unknown valley, seeing that none of us had ever been down in the Valais."

Little though they knew it they had made Alpine history for the point which they had reached - the Kungsfelsen, 4277m - was a height record for 8 years until the 24 year old Jacques Balmat beat them on Mont Blanc at 6.30pm on 8 August 1786.

The 'Magnificent Seven' are commemorated in a statue at Gressoney-St.-Jean - Valentin and Joseph Beck, Sebastian Linty,

Giovanni Nicolas Vincent, Stefan Litschgi (though some say Etienne Lisgie), Franz Castell and Joseph Zumstein. The statue is in the trees between the car park and the public toilets next to the river on the N side of the main road.

Many years later this frontier ridge was traversed to the great snowy plateau to the N, first by Joseph Zumstein and Johann Nicholas Vincent (son of the hero of 1778) with Mollinatti and A. Vincent on 1 August 1820, when on their way with a party of 13 people (!) up the Punta Zumstein/Zumsteinspitze, 4563m. [J. N. Vincent had climbed his Pyramide Vincent, 4215m, on 5 August 1819, solo, the peak being the lowest and the first ascended of the group of seven tops which constitute the Monte Rosa. Vincent and Zumstein together repeated the ascent a week later, with more favourable weather. On both, and subsequent ascents of the peaks from this side, the old gold mine workings on the Stolemberg peak were used for overnight shelter before the summit ascents].

Second to come this way was Signor Giovanni Gnifetti in August 1842 on his way to the conquest of the Punta Gnifetti/Signalkuppe, 4559m, on his fourth attempt at that peak over a period of eight years. [Curé Giovanni Gnifetti of Alagna first attempted the Punta Gnifetti on 27 July 1834, but bad weather prevented him reaching the summit. His second attempt was on 28-29 July 1836 when the lack of an ice axe within half an hour of the top stopped him going any further. Bad weather again foiled the third attempt on 12-13 August 1839 but he finally reached the top on 8-9 August 1842].

No one actually *crossed* the pass of the Colle del Lys/Lysjoch, 4248m, until it was traversed by William Matthews and his brother George St. John Matthews on 23 August 1859 with Jean Baptiste Croz and M. Charlet. They had the day before climbed up from Zermatt and stayed overnight at the Riffelberg Inn, which had been opened in 1854. The next day they crossed over the Lysjoch and descended to Gressoney-St.-Jean, where they stayed at the Pension Delapierre.

"The Italian valleys at our feet were filled with clouds, but we could just see underneath the roof of mist which covered the Val de Lys, and

183

trace the line of the silver Lys, winding through meadows of delicious green ... We were now enjoying the soft climate of Italy and the exquisite verdure and beautiful scenery (of the valley). Lofty cliff and noble pine forest, and foaming torrent, and huge erratic blocks, islands in a sea of green, were here thrown together by the hand of nature in exhaustless variety and profusion; and the affect of all this natural beauty is increased by the apparent comfort of the dwellings, and the bright and picturesque costume of the inhabitants. We reached Gressoney-St.-Jean, with its cluster of white houses and elegant Italian campanile, situated in the midst of verdant meadows, on the banks of the foaming Lys."

At about the time of this excursion the Rev. S. W. King and his wife were enjoying the hospitality of the Baron Louis Pecoz at his hunting lodge *"...where Delapierre brought them the tidings of the fact that two Englishmen"* (the Matthews brothers) *"had reached Gressoney... by way of the snow plateau between Mont Rosa and the Liskamm. At this absurd announcement the Baron burst into a healthy fit of laughter, evidently relishing the joke that Delapierre had been made the victims of such a hoax..."* The Baron was sceptical that such a feat would be possible, but Rev. King and Delapierre so persuaded the Baron that the next day they climbed up to the pass and could see for themselves the track that the Matthews had made.

The Matthews account of 1859 was not published until 1862 (in Wm. Matthews *'Peaks, Passes and Glaciers'*) but once the passage of the Lysjoch was opened by Matthews, other travellers were not slow to take advantage of the new route. For example, in the following year alone, there were three recorded ascents to the col:

13 August 1860: Rev. Leslie Stephen and Robert Liveing, with Melchior Andegg, climbed the Zumsteinspitze from the N side, making the first ascent of the peak since Zumstein's last ascent in 1822.

Also on 13 August 1860: E. B. Prest, J. L. Propert and an American J. K. Stone, with Johann zum Taugwald, Moritz Andermatten and one of the Simonds from Chamonix crossed from Riffelberg to Gressoney.

On 29 August 1860 the Rev. T. G. Bonney and J. C. Hawkshaw

with Michel Croz, visited the col from the Riffelberg.

In 1861 Messrs. William Matthews and F. W. Jacomb discovered a lower but more difficult pass from the Riffel to the Val de Lys. This is the Felikjoch, 4016m, between Liskamm and Castor. The valley is reached by going across the Felik glacier to the CAI Rifugio Quintino Sella. The Lysjoch was also crossed by Tuckett on 15 June 1861 with C. H. and W. F. Fox and J. J. Bennen and Peter Perren, from Riffelberg to Gressoney, and from the Lysjoch on 19 August 1861 a large party, headed by the Rev. J. Frederick Hardy, were the first to climb Liskamm, 4527m, in 3hr from the pass.

On 25 August 1894 the Queen of Italy crossed the pass from Gressoney to Zermatt with a caravan of 30 persons, led by Alessandro Welf of Gressoney, under the general direction of Baron Louis Pecoz. On the descent Baron Pecoz collapsed of a heart attack and died. His body was taken down to Zermatt on 28 August and the next day conveyed by a special train to Visp, thence back to Italy over the Simplon.

Both the Lysjoch and the Felikjoch (on the E and W sides of Liskamm respectively) were two of the most frequented passes crossed by British prisoners of war who escaped from Italian prison camps in the confusion which followed the fall of Mussolini. Those who were fortunate crossed the Swiss frontier near the shores of Lakes Maggiore and Lugano, but hundreds were forced to attempt the glacier passes. In the autumn of 1943 some 1600 men reached Switzerland by these passes, the Breuiljoch (beneath Mont Cervino), the Monte Moro and other passes, and 1500 more crossed the passes in the Simplon region. Few accounts of these crossings were written and few records kept.

The crossing of the Lysjoch is an easy expedition, but it is very laborious if the snow is soft.

The pass commands, as might be expected from its great height, a glorious view. The mountaineer looks S upon the great plains of Piedmont, enclosed by the Ligurian Apennines and the curving line of the Mantine and Cottian Alps, from which, at a distance of nearly 100 miles, rises the noble pyramid of Monte Viso. In the immediate

185

foreground is the broad eastern arm of the Lys glacier bounded on the W by a long spur of the Liskamm and on the E by the line of peaks from the Parotspitze to the Pyramide Vincent.

The Valle di Gressoney and the Monte Rosa peaks

SECTION 6.2
The NAME of MONTE ROSA

W.A.B. Coolidge in his *'Alpine Studies'* says that the history of the name of Monte Rosa is intricate and confused and not as easy to place as Mont Blanc, its loftier rival. He based his difficulty on two facts:
1. That Monte Rosa rises on a political frontier, which was not the case of Mont Blanc until 1860, and
2. That Monte Rosa is composed of a number of summits of nearly equal height, whereas Mont Blanc and its immediate satellites tower hugely over its neighbours.

Coolidge says that the alpine historian has to bear in mind:
a) That a pass almost always was named before its neighbouring peaks;
b) It was the pass which frequently gave its name to the peak, and not the reverse, as became generally the case in the mid-19thC;
c) A special name was generally first bestowed on a mountain range of greater or lesser extent;
d) The name then shifted about from peak to peak within that range, and then;
e) The name finally settled on the highest summit.

Coolidge's researches showed that the name Monte Rosa was:
1. First given to a pass, next to a peak W of that pass (Matterhorn);
2. As time went on, the name was given to the entire mountain group that rises E of the same pass, till finally;
3. The wandering name passed gradually from the Breithorn (at the W end of that snow-clad mass) over a still higher summit (the Liskamm) to rest on the real highest portion of the group.

Thus:
1. We have seen in the St. Théodule how this pass was first given the name in the 16thC 'Glacier' by the Valaisans, but 'Rosa' (or ruize, roise, roësa, rosio and roisa) by the men of Aosta.
2. By the turn of the 16thC the Matterhorn became known as 'M. Servino' or Matten M' but the great Swiss cartographer J.J. Scheuchzer

of Zurich fails to mention not only 'M. Rosa' but also the St. Théodule or the Matterhorn: it has been assumed that he never personally visited the Valais.

The first mention of Monte Rosa as a mountain *range* is in S. S. Gruner's book of 1760 and subsequent maps of the late 18thC apply 'the Rosa and its satellites' to the watershed between the Valais and the Duchy of Milan. As if to confirm those latest observations H. B. de Saussure himself gave the name Mont Rose to the group of peaks he could see from the Pedriolo hut near Macugnaga, which he visited in the summer of 1789.

3.   By the very end of the 18thC 'Mont Rose' had settled on the range, but in the early 19thC the name shifted about from one peak to another several times:

1800   George Cade's party, the first composed of Englishmen to cross the St. Théodule, could *"see the Mont Rose"* rising from the pass - a reference to the Breithorn.

1813   The Breithorn was ascended by the Frenchman Henri Maynard, with his guide M. J. Couttel. Couttel had been with de Saussure in 1792 up to the Klein Matterhorn and at that time de Saussure had named the Breithorn as Mont Rose. Couttel's mistake was recorded by Maynard.

1830   The Earl of Minto's party descended the Breithorn with M. Couttel (who had been up the peak with Sir John Herschel in 1821 and 1822), the son of old M. J. Couttel (of 1813). Lord Minto naturally used the name 'Monte Rosa' given to him by Couttel Junior.

1840   Messrs. Agassiz, Desor and Englehardt variously, in books and maps, give the name Mont Rose to the true Liskamm.

The Monte Rosa Peaks and their Ascent

1801   Punta Giordani, 4046m.

First climbed by Dr. Pietro Giordani of Alagna, this solitary ascent of a virgin 4000m peak being one of the outstanding achievements in the early history of mountaineering.

1816   Parotspitze, 4436m.   Dr. Frederic Parrot.

1819   Pyramide Vincent, 4214m.   Johann Niklaus Vincent, owner of the gold mines around Alagna, on 5 August 1819, solo.

1820   Zumsteinspitze, 4561m.   Joseph Zumstein, Mollinatti, A. Vincent and J. N. Vincent on 1 August 1820.

1822   Ludwigshöhe, 4340m.   Ludwig, Baron von Welden, Colonel of the Imperial Staff in Vienna. Von Welden's explorations of 1821-2 enabled him to give names to all but two of the ten summits of the Monte Rosa group.

1842   Punta Gnifetti/Signalkuppe, 4559m.   Pastor Giovanni Gnifetti, on 8-9 August 1842.

1855   Höchste Spitze/Dufourspitze, 4634m.   Ascended on 31 July 1855 by Messrs. J. G. and C. Smythe, Rev. Charles Hudson, John J. Birkbeck and E. J. Stephenson with Ulrich Lauener of Lauterbrunnen and Johannes zum Taugwald and two other Zermatt guides.

The highest peak was still known as the Höchste Spitze until it was named Dufourspitze by the Swiss Government on 28 January 1863 in honour of G. H. Dufour (1787-1875), Director General of the Swiss Survey.

It is indeed remarkable that, with the exception of Nord End, 4609m, and Dufourspitze, all the main summits of Monte Rosa were conquered before the beginnings of systematic mountaineering in the 1850s.

The first to traverse the whole arête from the frontier ridge to the highest summit were Messrs. Richard and William M. Pendlebury and the Rev. Charles Taylor, direct from Macugnaga, on 22 July 1872. The first Italian traverse of the summit was accomplished by a future Pope, Monsignor Achille Ratti, later Pope Pious XI, in 1889 from Macugnaga to Zermatt.

The best headquarters for all expeditions on the S side of the Monte Rosa massif is the CAI Rifugio Gnifetti. The frontier watershed can be reached without difficulty by the E side of the E arm of the Lys glacier and from the pass most of the minor summits of Monte Rosa, from the Parotspitze northwards, can be climbed directly in 1hr or less.

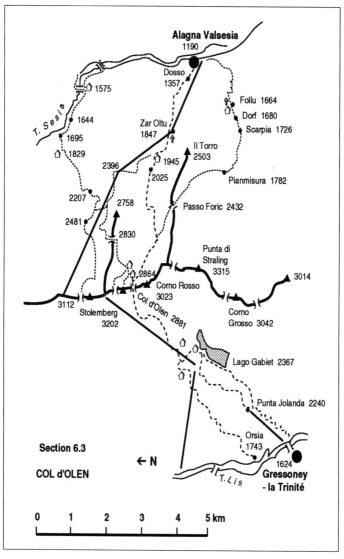

Alagna Valsesia
1190

Dosso
1357

Follu 1664

Dorf 1680

Scarpia 1726

1575

Zar Oltu
1847

Il Torro
2503

T. Sesia

1644

1695

1829

2396

1945

2025

Pianmisura 1782

2207

2758

Passo Foric 2432

2481

2830

Punta di
Straling
3315

3014

2864

Corno Rosso
3023

Col d'Olen 2881

Corno
Grosso 3042

3112

Stolemberg
3202

Lago Gabiet 2367

Punta Jolanda 2240

Section 6.3

COL d'OLEN

← N

Orsia
1743

1624

Gressoney
- la Trinité

T. Lis

0   1   2   3   4   5 km

SECTION 6.3
COL d'OLEN, 2881m

Distance: 13km, Gressoney-la-Trinité to Alagna
Height Gain: 1257m
Height Loss: 1691m
Grade: 3***

Outward		G.B.T.	Return	
		Gres'ney-la-Trinité, 1624m	6hr 30	1hr
1hr 30	1hr 30	Punta Jolanda, 2240m	5hr 30	30min.
45min.	2hr 15	Alpe Gabiet, 2342m	5hr	1hr
1hr 40	3hr 55	Col d'Olen, 2881m	4hr	4hr
3hr	6hr 55	Alagna, 1190m		

The principal ascent to the Col d'Olen starts at Orsia, 1743m, 1km N of Gressoney-la-Trinité on Path No.6 to Alpe Gabiet, but the walk has now been spoiled by being largely submerged under the pistes and ski roads of the Staffa-Orsia-Gabiet ski system. However, the views up the valley to Zwillinge and Liskamm are superb compensation. The ascent this way takes 3hr.

The former Orsia-Gabiet cable car has now been replaced by a new telecabine system starting at Staffa, to reach the Gabiet alp near the CAI Rifugio Lys (from where you can continue on foot to the Col d'Olen). The alternative is to start from Gressoney-la-Trinité itself. At Edelboden, on the E side of la-Trinité, a chairlift carries you steeply up to Punta Jolanda, 2240m, and saves a stiff climb of 1hr 30min. up the wooded slopes on Path No.5. From here it is just a 120m climb to Alpe Gabiet: there are two paths, waymarked Nos.5B and 5 respectively, and both take about 45min.

At Punta Jolanda the paths diverge, signposted Lago Nord and Lago Sud. Do not be misled into thinking that these two paths take you on the N or the S banks of the Lago Gabiet: they don't.

The Lago Nord path takes you on a northerly line, not marked on the Swiss LK maps, W of the Cime del Lago ridge - easily graded and giving superb views up the Lys valley to the Breithorn. In places it follows bulldozed tracks, but in other parts it follows a moraine-like edge of debris, quite delightful. The path is good throughout.

The Lago Sud path, No.5, involves some climbing to get up to cross the S ridge of the Cime del Lago, but then it follows an old railway line (used for the construction of the Lago Gabiet barrage) for c1km to the dam, and then follows a path on the NW side of the lake. At the Alp del Lago bear away from the lake to the Alpe Gabiet. On this route there are no views up to the frontier peaks.

[An alternative to the Punta Indren/Path No.5 route is to follow the Gabiet stream from Edelboden to its source at the lake. At Edelboden Inferiore (the chalets opposite the road junction to Gressoney) take Path No.3, becoming Path No.4, up the L flank of the Gabiet glen, passing a waterfall and reaching the barrage of Lago Gabiet in 1hr 30min. Climb up the W end of the dam and follow Path No.5 along the W shore of the lake to Alpe Gabiet].

On the Alpe Gabiet, 2342m, between the lake and the cablecar station, is a large two-storey stone building, the former CAI Rifugio Gabiet, now privately run. Just above the cablecar station is the private Albergo delle Ponte, while just across from the cablecar station is the CAI Rifugio Lys 'Gallarate', 2358m, a small whitewashed building inaugurated by the CAI on 8 September 1946, although the building dates from 1906.

Where the Staffa télécabine ends at the Alpe Gabiet (and where the bubble cars take the next stage to Passo dei Salati, 2936m, for those going mountaineering), chairlifts take over to about the 2750m contour (not operating in summer). Path No.6 follows a jeep track at first, passing the remains of railways and cableways in the upper part of the combe, remains of the 18th-19thC gold mining operations, but then you can see faint waymarks alongside a stream taking a direct line. The path crosses the jeep track and climbs a spur overlooking the Indren valley, and there are superb views up to the Pyramide Vincent and Liskamm. You can see summer skiers on the Indren

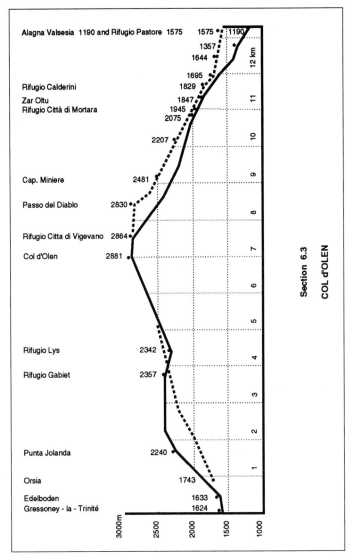

Alagna Valsesia 1190 and Rifugio Pastore 1575 — 1575 · 1190

1357
1644

1695
Rifugio Calderini — 1829
Zar Oltu — 1847
Rifugio Città di Mortara — 1945
2075

2207

Cap. Miniere — 2481

Passo del Diablo — 2830

Rifugio Citta di Vigevano — 2864

Col d'Olen — 2881

Rifugio Lys — 2342

Rifugio Gabiet — 2357

Punta Jolanda — 2240

Orsia — 1743

Edelboden — 1633
Gressoney - la - Trinité — 1624

Section 6.3
COL d'OLEN

glacier or climbers crossing it to the CAI Rifugio Giovanni Gnifetti or the smaller CAI Rifugio Città di Mantova.

From the top station of the chairlift the waymarked path scrambles over slaty rock and through snow patches to the crest of the pass. The pass is marked by a tatty Italian flag (an indicator for the nearby CAI Rifugio) and a Madonna shrine. There is no shelter.

The old Albergo de Col d'Olen, 2880m, is seen from the pass, 2 min. away to the E. This large and once comfortable inn was built in 1878 and afforded excellent headquarters for exploring the Monte Rosa range. It is now the privately-run Rifugio Guglielmina, competing for accommodation with the nearby and equally impressive CAI Rifugio Città di Vigevano, 2864m, 100 metres beyond, 5min. from the Col on its E side and 5m lower. This was built in 1914 as the Albergo Stolemberg-Grober and was acquired by the CAI in 1947. The Lago di Varese - one of the Italian Lakes - is visible from its windows.

From the Colle, but better seen from the Rifugio Vigevano, is the ridge of summits bounding the E side of the Val Sesia which we need to cross the next day. Prominent is the massive flat-topped Monte Tagliaferro, 2964m, and to its R, beyond the subsidiary peak of Dosso Grinner, 2761m, is the Bochetta della Moanda, 2422m. To the L of the Tagliaferro is the pass of Colle Mud, 2324m, then the fine steep cone of Corno Mud, 2802m. Next is the Colle Piglimo, 2485m, and then after the rocky crest of Corno Piglimo, 2894m, is the Turlo Pass, 2738m, with its mule track prominently seen.

There are many paths around the Rifugio Vigevano. An easy stroll (Path No.56) is up the Corno del Camoscio/Gemshorn, 3026m, a half-hour climb. Some say that the view that it commands of the great range is preferable even to that from the Testa Grigia/Groshaupt. The Rev. King was certainly enthusiastic.

Another path (Path No.5) leads round the E side of the Camoscio to the edge of the Indren glacier in 1hr 30min. passing Turin University's A. Mosso Scientific Institute at 2900m, en route to the Passo Dei Salati, 2936m (and the top of the gondola lift from Gabiet), and to the Stolemberg peak, 3202m, and the Colle delle Pisse, 3112m.

From the Col d'Olen there are three ways down to Val Sesia -

6.3.1.   The descent on Path Nos.5C/5 is for some time down rather steep and stony slopes and then along a barren valley following the Olen stream, past the Grande Halte chalets, 1945m, where there is the CAI Rifugio Città di Mortara (1hr 15min. from the Col), then to the Zar Oltu chalets, 1847m, and the Alagna-Indren cablecar station, then by a steep zig-zag path through the delightful group of chalets at Dosso, 1357m, and down into Alagna.

6.3.2.   Path No. 5E traverses NW of the Laghetti Cimalegna then NE to reach in 15min. a cairn at 2830m on a ridge, marking the Passo del Diavolo.   Go down the N side, steeply at first, on Path No.10B, sometimes traversing, to reach the bed of a dried up lake in the Stolemberg combe at a point underneath the Alagna-Indren cableway. Follow the stream flowing from the Stolemberg slopes and pick up a path at Capanna Miniere, 2481m, (a relic from gold mining days) and down to the Alpe la Barma, 2207m.   Continue on Path No.10 down into the Bors glen in 30min. to Alpe Bors, 1829m, and the CAI Rifugio Anna Crespi Calderini on the lip of the hanging valley. This rifugio is very small and has restricted opening days: it will be best to continue to the CAI Rifugio Francesco Pastore to be assured of a bed and be in a better position to tackle the Col del Turlo (or other northern passes) next day.   Therefore continue on Path No.10, becoming Path No.6, down the main valley to the Rifugio Pastore at Alpe Pile, 1575m.

[Alternatively, from the dried up lake in the Stolemberg coomb go E on a path to a supporting tower of the Alagna-Indren cableway, c2480m, and traverse round the Vallone dell Pisse on Path No.10B to reach the cablecar station at Bocheta della Pisse, 2396m.

Here there are further choices:

a) descend by cablecar via Zar Oltu to Alagna;

b) descend Path No.5A via CAI Rifugio Città di Mortara at the Grande Halte (or Alt) chalets on Alpe Seiwji, 1945m, thence to Alagna via the road from Zar Oltu;

c) or by Path Nos. 10D and 5F, round the N side of Cornu d'Olen, 2556m, via Stofful to Alagna].

6.3.3. Instead of descending Path No.5 all the way down the Valle d'Olen turn off R below the Sasso del Diavolo on Path No.3B to the grassy Passo Foric, 2432m, and follow a good path SE to reach the Alpe di Pianmisura chalets. The larger group - Grande - are across the Rio Foric to the W at 1854m, the altitude of the white-fronted Chapel of Madonna della Névé, built in 1737. We arrive at the smaller group - Piccolo - at 1782m. One chalet here is dated 1893.

Path No.3 turns R, SE, and at the treeline passes through the delightful Walser settlements hamlets in the Valle d'Otro where the huge wooden houses integrate perfectly with their pastoral surroundings - past Scarpia, 1726m, Dorf, 1680m, (though signs say 1640m and maps say 1698m) (toilets 100 metres along the track here) and Follu, 1664m, (where there is the Restaurant Alpino and a chapel dated 1659).

The Vallone d'Otro was given in 1028 by Corrado di Salico to Peter, Bishop of Novara, and by 1184 by Pope Lucio III to the Monastery of San Pietro in Castelletto. Although the valley has been settled for c2000 years it is noted for its Walser hamlets, built by the Savoyards who settled in the area from 1636. A most interesting time can be spent looking round the chalets, marvelling at their method of construction.

At the edge of the meadow beyond Follu there begins a steep descent through woods of fir, birch and beech into the main valley. The path passes, at $^1/_3$ and $^2/_3$ in distance/time, two chapels, two or three shrines and two water points. The path is well maintained, indicating the popularity of the walk to the Otro settlements. When the path crosses a dirt road go straight across and follow the path all the way through Riale (on the S edge of Alagna) and emerge in Alagna's square on its S side at a point between a water trough and the statue of Antonio Grober (1847-1909).

The Col d'Olen and descent to Alagna

Forbes passed over the Col d'Olen in 1842 having climbed up to the Lys glacier the day before to make observations. He ascended in 2hr 15min. from Stavel, a good rate of ascent.

The Rev. King also came this way on 24 September 1855, accompanied by Zumstein, with whom he had stayed and travelled for a few days. They found the ascent, by steep green slopes past Orsia and Bédémie and the Gabiet alp, not difficult. They ascended the Gemshorn *"- a lofty exposed ridge of rock -"* for the view.

"The view was superbly grand. ...Directly before us, with a wide valley of desolation intervening, was the colossal butt-end of Monte Rosa in full face, with its rugged bases, and enormous pyramids of dark rock and cold dreamlike glaciers of incalculable extent; their frozen billows rent and crevassed, foaming down its deeply furrowed flank between huge overhanging cliffs; which were crowned by the glistening dome of the Höhelicht, the Liskamm, and the Vincent Pyramide. A large rounded rock, halfway down from the Höhelicht, was an interesting object, being the spot where stood Vincent's cabin during his gold mining operations and Zumstein's ascents of Monte Rosa. Behind us, the sunless crags of the north side of the Weisshorn, savage and repellent in all aspects, were covered with fresh snow. To the W, the dark depths of the Val de Lys seemed as if light and warmth could never penetrate the profound chasm, shut in by many a familiar line of lofty Alps; ... over the dark line which marked the Val d'Aosta rose Mont Emilius and the lofty points between the Vals

Tournanche and Ayas with the "saphire-hued pyramid of Mont Viso" and beyond all the summits of Mont Blanc in the far distance ... barely rising above the seried crest of mountains. In utter contrast to all this, far to the east lay the sunny land of Italy; on which - beyond bare ridges of deep brown, olive-green, and purpled peaks, shutting out the apparently still and lifeless valley - we once more beheld the blue expanse of Lago Maggiore, among the far-spreading plains of Lombardy, marked with the silvery lines of large rivers, and the glistening clusters of Milan, Novara, and innumerable towns and villages; backed by the far distant ranges of the Grissons and the Tirol and, towering above all, the huge Ortler Spitze."

From the Col d'Olen both Forbes and King descended to Alagna by what is now Path Nos.5C/5. Forbes described his descent: *"From a little way beyond the Col* [from where the Rifugio Città di Vigevano now stands] *there is a fine view eastwards, including part of the Lago Maggiore and the hills beyond. The descent to Alagna is very steep and long (as it lies much lower than Gressoney), but, at the same time, interesting.*

"The Val Sesia is here very narrow, and is included between serrated chains of mountains, of which the Punta di Straling, 3115m, on the western, and the Tagliaferro, 2964m, and the Monte Turlo, 3128m, on the eastern side are conspicuous.

"The lower part of the descent to Alagna is through beautiful woods and green pastures. Alagna itself has a pretty church, in the Italian taste, and is most agreeably situated."

On arrival at Alagna, Forbes called on the priest, Giovanni Gnifetti who, on 9 August 1842 - only a few days before Forbes' visit - had ascended the Punta

Gnifetti.

The Rev. King also described the steep and rough descent from the Col in 1855 and noted that *"...many of the rocks were of a fine green serpentine, and at a little distance, were the ruins of miners' huts and the indications of the deserted copper and gold mines. ...The last descent to Alagna was through woods of beech, alder, cherry, maple and other deciduous trees, the site of which was most refreshing."*

Having reached Alagna King found *"...the change from one side of the Col to the other was at once manifest; we were not only in Italy, but Italian was spoken by all, as well as German (Alagna being one of the German colonies); and it was a pleasure to exchange the wretched French patois intermingled with Romansch, as spoken in the Vals we had been traversing, for intelligible though anything but pure Italian."*

Rifugio Francesco Pastore at Alpe Pile, 1575m

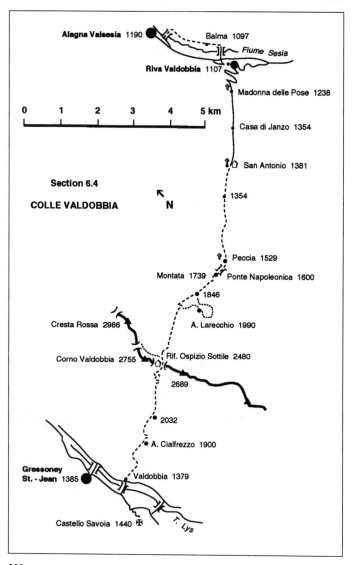

SECTION 6.4
COLLE VALDOBBIA, 2480m

Distance:	15.2km, Gressoney-St.-Jean to Riva
Height Gain:	1122m
Height Loss:	1400m
Grade:	3**

Outward		G.B.T.	Return	
		Gres'-St.-Jean, 1385m	5hr 30	15min.
15min.	15min.	Valdobbia, 1379m	5hr 15	45min.
1hr 30	1hr 45	A. Cialfrezzo Sotto, 1900m	4hr 30	45min.
1hr 30	3hr 15	Colle Valdobbia, 2480m	3hr 45	2hr 15
1hr	4hr 15	Ponte Napoleonica, 1600m	1hr 30	45min.
45min.	5hr	San Antonio, 1381m	45min.	15min.
15min.	5hr 15	Casa di Janzo, 1354m	30min.	30min.
30min.	5hr 45	Riva Valdobbia, 1107m		

Walkers leaving the Gressoney valley bound for the Val Sesia who are deterred by bad weather or fear of fatigue from attempting other routes may choose this easier but less interesting way by the Colle Valdobbia. Except for the botanist, who will find many rare plants by the way, this pass offers less of interest than most of those in the neighbourhood: yet the views of the Val de Lys from the W side, and of the Graian Alps and Gran Paradiso from the top of the Colle, are very fine. The pass was considered by the Rev. King to be of little interest compared with the Col d'Olen, but since then the aproaches to the Col d'Olen have been scarred by ski developments, to a similar extent as to the Colle di Bettaforca, but not to such an extent as the Cime Bianche routes.

The ascent towards the Colle begins a little below Gressoney-St.-

Jean at Valdobbia, 1327m, and is well marked by a formerly well-frequented mule path, No.11, very steeply up through the larch woods up to a clearing on a spur at 1850m in 1hr. From here there is a good view down to the Castello Savoia and across to the Colle della Ranzola. Turn the spur and continue through the woods, in 30min. to Alpe Cialfrezzo di Sotto, 1900m, and reach open ground. Cross the Torrente Valdobbia and climb up an old lateral moraine to the hidden Alpe Cialfrezzo do Sopra, 2023m, from where you can see the pass on the skyline ahead. The path then climbs more easily, but with the usual final steep climb across scree to reach the top.

There is a two-storey stone hospice on the summit of the pass, at 2480m. The pass was much frequented by travellers and herdsmen and this was the motive for constructing a chapel and stable on the pass in 1787. The present building is the work of Canon Nicolao Sottile and was completed on 22 July 1832. The hospice became, on 7 September 1871, a meteorological observatory, but that use has ceased and the hospice is now the CAI Rifugio Ospizio Sottile. It has basic accommodation for 20 and meals are available if required. The rifugio is a miserable place, but useful in emergency. The chapel is built into the hospice - the door is on the RHS: if it is closed ask the guardian to open it for you to see the huge carved wooden altar pieces and sculpture.

On the E side of the Colle Valdobbia the path descends in a straight line NE as Path No.1 to the Alpetto pastures (where a diversion R, on Path No. 1A, well worth the detour, leads to the lake and chalets of Alpe Larecchio, 1900m, in a delightful basin) then passes through the remains of an old pine forest before reaching Montata, 1739m, a small hamlet much destroyed by a violent fire in 1899. The Cappella of the Madonna of the Snows here was rebuilt in 1991. From Montata descend steeply to the Torrente Solivo and the old pack-horse bridge of Ponte Napoleonica, 1600m.

Here Path No.1 joins the main Val Vogna. The delightful Torrente Vogna tumbles down a wooded glen from the Colle del Maccagno, 2495m, and is followed by the GTA (Grande Traversata della Alpi) on its way to Alagna and onwards to either Macugnaga or Carcoforo.

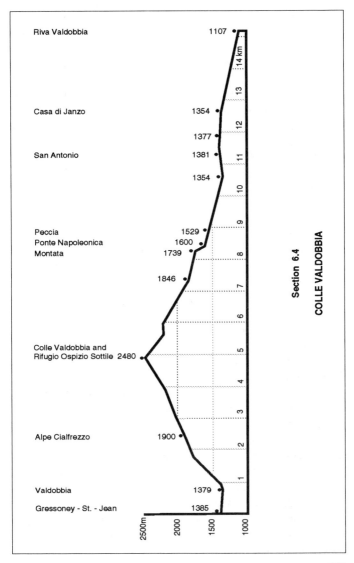

Riva Valdobbia — 1107 — 14 km
13
Casa di Janzo — 1354 — 12
— 1377 —
San Antonio — 1381 — 11
— 1354 — 10
9
Peccia — 1529
Ponte Napoleonica — 1600
Montata — 1739 — 8
— 1846 — 7
6
Colle Valdobbia and
Rifugio Ospizio Sottile — 2480 — 5
4
3
Alpe Cialfrezzo — 1900 — 2
1
Valdobbia — 1379
Gressoney - St. - Jean — 1385
2500m   2000   1500   1000

Section 6.4
COLLE VALDOBBIA

Ascents from the Colle Valdobbia

The Colle is popularly used for those intending to climb the Corno di Valdobbia and the Corno Bianco.

The **Corno di Valdobbia, 2775m,** is easily reached up its S ridge from the pass in 45min.

For the **Corno Bianco, 3320m,** drop down the E side of the pass for 30m to find a faint path (signposted) northwards as Path No.1B to the Passo di Valdobbiola, 2635m, on a commodious path beneath the E face of the Corno di Valdobbia. Continue northwards on the W flank of the Cresta Rossa, overlooking Gressoney-St.-Jean, to the Passo dell'Alpetto, 2774m. From here descend NE on Path No.2D to the Lago Nero and climb steeply up 200m or so to the Passo d'Artemisia. From the Rifugio Sottile the ascent of Corno Bianco takes about 4hr 30min. - 5hr. This is a serious route for mountaineers only.

Chapel of San Grato, Peccia, 1529m, Val Vogna

From the Ponte Napoleonica the view downstream through the larches in the gorge leads the eye to the stone tower of the chapel of San Grato, at 1529m, marking the edge of the hamlet of Peccia, reached in 5min. The chapel, plain and locked, has a tablet which says: *At this spot, on 13 February 1870, Giacomo Clerino, aged 76, the first custodian of Ospizio Sottile, whilst helping 4 wayfarers overcome by cold in a blizzard when showing them the way to the pass, was buried beneath an avalanche and died. - One hundred years later Riva Valdobbia showed that he had not been forgotten.*

Amongst the farm buildings in Peccia at 1449m are the shrines of Cappella di San Marco and also San Nicolao.

Thirty minutes beyond Peccia, Path No.2 from Lago Bianco and the Passo di Rissuolo and Passo del Alpetto come in from the L then you reach the footbridge at 1351m where the Vogna falls into a deepand dramatic gorge. In a few more minutes you reach a shrine (water) and the hamlet of San Antonio at the roadhead (1381m).

The Oratorio di Sant'Antonio of Padova was built in 1604 and contains a crucifix in the Baroque style and a late-18thC mural. Opposite is the modest but comfortable private Rifugio Valle Vogna, having a bar and restaurant, open from 1 April to 30 November.

The road begins a long and easy descent high above the Torrente Vogna, passing Casa Morca, 1378m, (small store, telephone) and Casa di Janzo, 1354m, then past the isolated chapel of Madonna delle Pose, 1238m. This was built in 1665 and has beside it a small chapel dedicated to local men who died in the First World War.

Just after the bend in the road beyond the church a gap in the bushes on the RHS reveals a path which avoids the final zig-zags of the road as it drops down to Riva. The path crosses the road again and soon, between two steel electricity poles, takes another gap on the RHS. Cross the road twice and go between large detached houses and in 15 min. you are on the S side of the parish church of San Michele & Maria Assunta, 1107m, in the Piazza 4 November.

It takes 45min. to walk the 2.5km up to Alagna for accommodation - there's none in Riva. Walk N up the village street, passing the Piazza Antonio Carestia on the LHS, and at the N side of the cemetery (many notable family shrines) take a private road down to the main road, cross it and then the Fiume Sesia (by a narrow bridge) to Balma. Take the path upstream and at the next bridge cross the river and main road again. Take another private road past a block of condominiums to emerge in Alagna's main street about 400 metres S of its centre.

Statue of Antonio Grober, President of the Italian Alpine Club from 1891 to 1909, in Alagna Valsesia

The Colle Valdobbia was crossed by both the Rev. King and Hinchliff in 1856 en route from Riva to Gressoney-St.-Jean and by Tuckett on 28 June 1856 from Gressoney-St.-Jean to Varallo. Tuckett also crossed the pass again five years later, on 17 June 1861, from Gressoney to Alagna and, in the same afternoon, crossed the Colle Mud to Rima, then descended the Sermenza to sleep at Rimasco - quite a day!

When Hinchliff came this way in 1856, in the reverse direction, he recorded: *"Early in the afternoon* (having come from Lake Maggiore and the Monte Moro) *we arrived at Rima, a miserable village, where however we resolved to sleep, with a view of crossing the Val Dobbia to Gressoney on the next day. The little inn was the worst we had stayed at in the course of our journey. ...*

"We started early in the morning, and crossed the Val Dobbia to Gressoney. This pass is certainly the most uninteresting I have seen, and I should strongly advise everyone to go to Alagna instead of stopping at Riva, and thence cross to Gressoney by the Col d'Olen, which, though somewhat more fatiguing, is infinitely more worth seeing, passing as it does, close to the foot of Monte Rosa and the Liskamm. At the highest point of the Val Dobbia is a miserable little building, dignified by the name of Hospice, where, however, we got some tolerable bread and cheese."

The next day Hinchliff wanted to go up the valley to Liskamm, but only got as far as the glacier before a rain storm turned him back. That night two Englishmen turned up at his inn at Gressoney, soaking wet, having crossed the Col de Ranzola from Brusson. The next day he accompanied them to the Col d'Olen, as they were going to Alagna, but he turned back within half an hour of the pass, having seen *"just enough to satisfy me that this pass must be an exceedingly fine one in good weather."* The next day the weather was better, and Hinchliff crossed over the Col de Ranzola to Brusson.

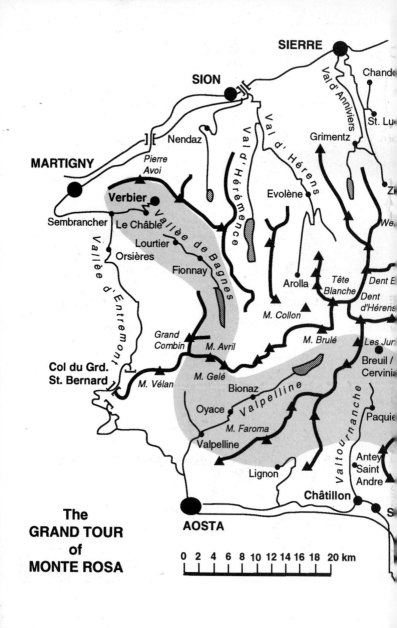

The
GRAND TOUR
of
MONTE ROSA

0 2 4 6 8 10 12 14 16 18 20 km